TIME
ANNUAL
2003

By the Editors of TIME

TIME
ANNUAL

BRAVO! Claudio Reyna, the U.S. captain, salutes American fans at soccer's World Cup

2003
By the Editors of TIME

CONTENTS

36

34

2

TIME ANNUAL 2003

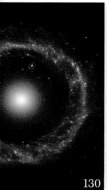
130

150

114

160

Cover photography credits:
Front cover, center: Brigitte Stelzer—Gamma. Front cover, top, from
left to right: Reuters—Landov; Brooks Kraft—Gamma for TIME;
Iraq News Agency—AP/Wide World; David McNew—Getty Images.
Back cover, clockwise from top left: Shannon Stapleton—Polaris;
NASA; Todd Kaplan—Starfile; Warren Zinn—U.S. Army Pool—Getty

LEFT TO RIGHT: JULIE JACOBSON—AP/WIDE WORLD; WARREN ZINN—U.S. ARMY POOL—
GETTY; CHARLIE RIEDEL—AP/WIDE WORLD; NASA; TODD KAPLAN—STARFILE;
SHAUN BOTTERILL—GETTY IMAGES; BETTMANN—CORBIS

THE TIME ANNUAL

TIME ANNUAL

MANAGING EDITOR	Kelly Knauer
DESIGNER	Lee Ellen Fanning
PICTURE EDITOR	Patricia Cadley
RESEARCH DIRECTOR/WRITER	Matthew McCann Fenton
PRODUCTION EDITOR	Michael Skinner
COPY EDITOR	Bruce Christopher Carr
INDEX	Marilyn Rowland

TIME INC. HOME ENTERTAINMENT

PRESIDENT	Rob Gursha
VICE PRESIDENT, BRANDED BUSINESSES	David Arfine
EXECUTIVE DIRECTOR, MARKETING SERVICES	Carol Pittard
DIRECTOR, RETAIL & SPECIAL SALES	Tom Mifsud
DIRECTOR OF FINANCE	Tricia Griffin
MARKETING DIRECTOR	Kenneth Maehlum
ASSISTANT MARKETING DIRECTOR	Ann Marie Doherty
PREPRESS MANAGER	Emily Rabin
BOOK PRODUCTION MANAGER	Jonathan Polsky
ASSOCIATE PRODUCT MANAGER	Sara Stumpf

SPECIAL THANKS TO:

Robert Dente, Gina Di Meglio, Anne-Michelle Gallero, Peter Harper, Suzanne Janso, Natalie McCrea, Jessica McGrath, Mary Jane Rigoroso, Steven Sandonato, Bozena Szwagulinski, Niki Whelan

THE WORK OF THESE TIME STAFF MEMBERS AND CONTRIBUTORS IS FEATURED IN THIS VOLUME:
Kathleen Adams, Leslie Berestein, Lisa Beyer, Amanda Bower, Jess Cagle, Massimo Calabresi, Kate Carcaterra, Margaret Carlson, James Carney, Howard Chua-Eoan, John Cloud, Wendy Cole, Richard Corliss, Jeanne DeQuine, Andrea Dorfman, John F. Dickerson, Michael Duffy, Jackson Dykman, Daniel Eisenberg, Michael Elliott, Philip Elmer-DeWitt, Christopher John Farley, Ed Gabel, Nancy Gibbs, Frederic Golden, Andrew Goldstein, Dan Goodgame, Christine Gorman, James Graff, Karl Taro Greenfeld, Lev Grossman, Jamil Hamad, Anita Hamilton, Rita Healy, Leon Jaroff, Daniel Kadlec, Aharon Klein, Jeffrey Kluger, Richard Lacayo, Michael D. Lemonick, Joe Lertola, Eugene Linden, Belinda Luscombe, Scott MacLeod, J.F.O. McAllister, Jeanne McDowell, Johanna McGeary, Jodie Morse, Michele Orecklin, Tim Padgett, Priscilla Painton, Alice Park, Alex Perry, James Poniewozik, Eric Pooley, Hugh Porter, Andrew Purvis, Paul Quinn-Judge, Amany Radwan, Romesh Ratnesar, Matt Rees, Amanda Ripley, Simon Robinson, George Russell, Richard Schickel, Elaine Shannon, Janice C. Simpson, Sora Song, Joel Stein, Rick Stengel, Ron Stodghill II, Jan Stojaspal, Robert Sullivan, Heather Won Tesoriero, Mark Thompson, Karen Tumulty, Lon Tweeten, Josh Tyrangiel, David Van Biema, Douglas Waller, Michael Weisskopf, Richard Zoglin

SPECIAL THANKS TO:
Ken Baierlein, Andy Blau, Howard Chua-Eoan, Barbara Dudley Davis, John Dragonetti, Richard Duncan, Jeffrey Duque, Arthur Hochstein, Edward L. Jamieson, Kevin Kelly, Joe Lertola, Kent Ochjaroen, Steve Pang, Richard K. Prue, Aleksey Razhba, Jennifer Roth, Michele Stephenson, Lamarr Tsufura, Miriam Winocour

2002 Images

A portfolio of
the year's most
memorable
photographs

**3/11/02: A pair of twin
towers of light—a tribute
to those who died six
months before—soar
high into the sky from
ground zero in Manhattan**

Photograph by Charlie Riedel—AP/Wide World

Dried Up by Drought, America's Forests Are Devoured by Flames

As America suffers through a summer of drought, wildfires imperil a house outside Durango, Colo. Though we associate such fires with the heavily timbered mountain regions of the West, dry weather across the nation touched off infernos in every continental state. By fall, the fires had destroyed almost 7 million acres, double the 10-year average. On a single day in July, 443 new fires were reported in the West. One of the worst of the blazes forced almost all of the 30,000 residents around Show Low, Ariz., to flee—and some 400 homeowners returned to find only smoldering ruins.

On Hallowed Ground, A Gathering Recalls Horror and Heroism

United Airlines flight attendants gather to pray outside Shanksville, Pa., where Flight 93 crashed on Sept. 11, 2001, killing 44 people, including four hijackers. In a moving ceremony in the small Allegheny mountain town, a bell tolled 40 times as the names of the 40 crash victims—including several reported to have actively thwarted the hijackers—were read. After the service, President Bush and the First Lady visited informally with relatives of the victims, many of whom spontaneously stood during the ceremony to turn and applaud the citizens of Shanksville—all 245 of them—for their support.

Michelangelo—Not. In Saddam's Iraq, Art Is Tyranny's Servant

A statue of Iraqi strongman Saddam Hussein presides over a sculptor's studio in Baghdad. In like fashion, Saddam's outsize profile loomed over the year 2002, as U.S. President George Bush branded him a terrorist, one who was assembling an arsenal of weapons of mass destruction. Saddam, said Bush, had to relinquish his stockpile of weapons—or the U.S. would do the job for him. Saddam is one of the last of the old-fashioned dictators who rule through the cult of personality and the implements of torture. If Bush's demand for a "regime change" in Iraq is realized in 2003, Baghdad's sculptors, one suspects, may welcome a change of subject.

Warring over Different Gods, Muslims and Hindus Battle in India

A group of Hindu pilgrims was returning by train from the disputed holy site of Ayodhya in the western Indian state of Gujarat when someone pulled the emergency brake. The train halted in a mostly Muslim neighborhood where a mob was waiting with stones, knives and gasoline. The horde burned the pilgrims' coaches and murdered 58 people, 40 of them women and children. In retaliation, a crowd of 2,000 Hindus rioted against Muslims in the area, leaving hundreds dead. The incident was only the most violent in a series of bloody religious clashes as Hindu India and Muslim Pakistan—ancient foes who are now novice nuclear powers—skirmished in a battle of nerves that came to the brink of war.

DCINC

Inside Centcom, Top U.S. Generals Plan a Battle Half a World Away

While U.S. troops were gearing up to launch Operation Anaconda in Afghanistan, military brass gave TIME photographer Christopher Morris a rare opportunity: to bypass strict security and record the strategists orchestrating the battle, General Tommy Franks and his Central Command team, at their headquarters at MacDill Air Force Base in Tampa, Fla. In this meeting, Commander in Chief Franks ("CINC," right center) briefs military staff from 27 allied nations. High-tech communications allow Franks and his team to monitor events and supervise strategy on battlefields more than 7,000 miles away.

How To Bridge a Chasm Between Cultures? Try Candy, Gifts and Smiles

The scene is familiar from a hundred World War II movies: the smiling serviceman, a fish out of water, surrounded by a gang of lovable local kids. The props are a given: candy and bubble gum. But this time around, the locale isn't a shattered European city but a street in West Kabul, Afghanistan. And the soldier is not an American G.I.; he is Scott Palmer, a British paratrooper serving with the international peacekeeping force. Photographer Yunghi Kim reports that the Afghan kids, awed by the British troops and impressed with their strangely colored hair, followed them around and communicated by signs. Who says there's no such thing as an international language?

O Unholy Night: Modern Woes Tarnish The Birthplace of Christ

It is a story as old as the Crusades, a tale of sanctuary and siege. For five weeks in the spring, some 250 Palestinians—gunmen, clerics and a few unarmed bystanders—sought refuge in the ancient Church of the Nativity, revered as the birthplace of Jesus. Outside, the sacred site was surrounded by Israeli troops, who had swarmed into Bethlehem in the wake of a deadly spate of Palestinian suicide attacks. After weeks of negotiation, and after eight of the Palestinians had been killed by Israeli gunfire, a truce was reached: the church bells rang and the Palestinians filed out. Thirteen of the men—long pursued by Israel—were sent into exile abroad.

Ooof! With a Show of Guts, America Joins World Soccer's Elite

Still smarting from their last-place finish in soccer's all-important World Cup in 1998, the U.S. team under Coach Bruce Arena set off for host nations Japan and South Korea determined to reach higher ground. And if that meant leaving the ground to block a penalty kick—as it did in this second-round match against bitter continental rival Mexico—well, ankles aweigh! From left, that's U.S. players John O'Brien, Pablo Mastroeni, team captain Claudio Reyna, Brian McBride and Tony Sanneh. Mexican kicker Cuauhtemoc Blanco is at lower right. The U.S. won the game, 2-0, and for the first time reached the quarterfinals of the Cup.

2/11/02

Big Air! Snowboarders Give the Games a New Mood and a New 'Tude

Ross Powers soars high over the half-pipe at the Olympic Games in Park City, Utah, on his way to a gold medal—and a clean sweep of the men's snowboarding event for the U.S. In its second Olympic appearance, the extreme sport jazzed up the august Games with a jolt of pure adrenaline. Forget *The Skater's Waltz:* Powers shredded to the blare of Metallica's *Whiskey in the Jar* and the Beastie Boys' *Fight for Your Right (to Party).* This lord of the board may be a party animal, but he's also a good guy. Powers, 23, who spent two years in leg braces to correct birth defects, runs a foundation to assist needy would-be boarders. Gnarly!

Photograph by David E. Klutho—*Sports Illustrated*

FACES IN THE NEWS

In the story of a year, sometimes the most indelible characters are those we've never met before— and may never encounter again

Coleen Rowley
Whistle Blower

One of the pioneers of women's fight to be treated as equals in the male-dominated culture of the FBI, Coleen Rowley joined the bureau in 1980 after earning a law degree and by 1995 was chief counsel in the Minneapolis field office. In May she wrote a 13-page letter to FBI Director Robert Mueller in which she accused the bureau of obstructing investigations that might have helped disrupt the 9/11 terrorist attacks. Rowley charged the FBI's top officials with having failed to allow the Minneapolis office permission to investigate Zacarias Moussaoui, the French-American operative who is facing trail for conspiracy in the attacks.

Charles Moose
Manhunter

Tracking a serial killer is tough enough. But for Charles Moose, 49, police chief of Montgomery County, Md., the desperate search to find the sniper who was shooting down innocent civilians around the nation's capital was played out on a vast public stage, with the eyes and ears of the world trained upon him. The onetime police chief of Portland, Ore., didn't bother to hide the anger he felt as the sniper's toll of victims mounted. "It's getting really, really personal now," he said on Oct. 7, when a 13-year-old middle-schooler was shot and critically wounded, the eighth of the D.C.-area victims. "Dear policeman," said a note written on a Tarot card and left at the scene, "I am God."

Moose was indeed taking the murders too personally, some experts charged; they felt his prey was enjoying the spectacle of a police chief in distress. The student's shooting, they pointed out, came after Moose said in public that the murderer had not yet attacked young people. The chief's wife Sandy, a lawyer, came to his defense: "He just cares so much that his passion is always coming into play." In the days that followed, Moose kept his feelings in check and began to develop a bizarre relationship with the unknown killers, who communicated with him via notes left at the scene of the slayings, even on the phone. As the pressure mounted, Moose remained a calming influence and a firm voice of authority. When two suspects were finally arrested on Oct. 24, citizens hung banners on local freeways that expressed the nation's feelings: THANKS, CHIEF MOOSE.

Daniel Pearl
Journalist

A bluegrass fiddler, a convivial and popular storyteller and the author of offbeat articles for the *Wall Street Journal*, Daniel Pearl was described by friends as a blithe, optimistic spirit. So it was not surprising that when the *Journal's* South Asia bureau chief set off on Jan. 23 for a meeting in Karachi with individuals who had promised him information about alleged shoe-bomber Richard Reid, Pearl was alone and unarmed. Three days later, Western news agencies received an e-mail that included four pictures of Pearl, 38, in captivity, sent by a group calling itself "the National Movement for the Restoration of Pakistani Sovereignty." Within weeks, Pakistani police traced the e-mail to three suspects; they fingered British-born Muslim radical Ahmad Omar Saeed Sheikh, 27. Arrested, Saeed confessed to the crime. But it was too late: a videotape of Pearl's murder—and beheading—was quickly found. Pearl's wife Mariane, a French journalist, gave birth to the couple's first child, Adam, in May. Saeed was sentenced to death in July.

Terry Barton
Fire Starter

In 2002 she became the most despised woman in Colorado, as hated as Mrs. O'Leary after her cow kick-started the Great Chicago Fire of 1871. The Hayman blaze southwest of Denver was an inferno that burned for 17 days, destroyed 100 homes and damaged $38 million in federal forest land. Who would have suspected that the part-time Forest Service agent who first reported the fire—and named it after a pioneer homestead—was also the person who started it? The story: Barton's marriage to husband John, whom friends described as abusive, had failed. She started the fire in the middle of the drought-parched woods in order to burn an old letter from him, she admitted in a plea bargain she reached early in December with federal prosecutors. As family friend Connie Work remarked, "Some things just get out of control." Indeed.

Sharbat Gula
Refugee

Seventeen years after readers first saw it, the image was still familiar: the young Afghan girl faced the camera with bright green eyes that seemed alive with unearthly intensity. The Pashtun tribeswoman had been photographed in 1984 at the Nasir Bagh refugee camp in Pakistan by Steve McCurry. Her parents were casualties of the Soviet war in Afghanistan; she was believed to be about 13 years old at the time. When her picture appeared on the cover of *National Geographic* magazine in 1985, it became an instant icon of the costs of war.

McCurry took the picture in the camp school and never learned the girl's name. As the years passed, he often showed the picture on his travels in the region and asked after her; this year his search ended when a man in Nasir Bagh recognized her. Sharbat Gula is now a baker's wife with three daughters of her own. Unlike millions of people on earth, she had never seen her famous portrait before this year.

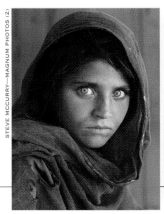 

Ronaldo
Athlete

For four years the world's best *futbol* player had lived in misery, haunted by the inexplicable medical seizure that had left him a walking zombie in Brazil's 3-0 loss to France in the finals of the 1998 World Cup. A plague of leg injuries had sidelined him in 2000-01. But in 2002 Ronaldo Luiz Nazario de Lima, 25, got himself a new haircut—albeit a strange one—and regained his old form. Brazil's team, which had lost an incredible six qualifying matches before the Cup, did the same: suddenly, "the beautiful game" was back, as Ronaldo and sidekicks Rivaldo and Ronaldinho passed the ball with anticipation that seemed telepathic. By the semifinals, Ronaldo had scored six goals. In the finals against Germany, he scored both goals in a 2-0 win—and the land of Pelé ruled again.

Kelly Clarkson
Idol

Today's most desired commodity—celebrity—came to a Texas cocktail waitress when viewers voted her the winner of the summer's big reality-TV hit, Fox's *American Idol*, an update of the *Amateur Hour* and *Star Search* shows. Will Clarkson, 20, parlay her 15 minutes of fame into a career? Stay tuned.

Snakehead
Channa argus

Yikes! The summer's best fish story involved a land-walking, air-breathing, rapidly migrating Chinese predator with gills, the snakehead. Its sighting in a Crofton, Md., pond in June sparked fears of a piscatorial disaster. Interior Secretary Gale Norton branded the critter "something from a bad horror movie" and declared she would seal the U.S. border against the Asian invader. Sadly for horror-movie fans, many experts deflated the claims made for the fish: it cannot live for three days without water, and its locomotion is a short, clumsy squirm rather than a fast walk.

Nia Vardalos
Filmmaker

Movie studios seldom produce in real life the kind of stories they routinely proffer on film—of heroic underdogs who triumph against all odds to beat the system. So imagine Hollywood's surprise when *My Big Fat Greek Wedding*, a "little" movie that cost only $5 million to make, became the biggest independent hit in history. *Wedding* opened in April, and the bells just kept ringing: by November it had grossed $185 million. The film began as a solo stage romp by Canadian-born comic Nia Vardalos, 39, based on her Greek heritage. After Tom Hanks and wife Rita Wilson (of Greek descent) saw the stage version, they bankrolled the film. Vardalos, a film novice, turned her personal history into an uproarious film with universal appeal. The surprised but irrepressible auteur told PEOPLE magazine, "I'm a boob job away from going L.A."

Steve Fossett
Adventurer

Some rich men collect paintings. Some collect wives. Steve Fossett collects records—no, not old Louis Armstrong recordings, but achievements that earn him a place in the annals of sport and adventure. Don't ask us what drives the 58-year-old investment tycoon from Chicago; we'll leave that to the psychologists. Before this year, Fossett had collected seven official world records for speed sailing. He had swum the English Channel and participated in the Iditarod. He had sailed across the Atlantic Ocean faster than any other human. He held the round-the-world speed record for medium-weight airplanes, as well as the U.S. transcontinental speed record for nonmilitary aircraft (no doubt a widely contested title). But Fossett's great grail of recent years still eluded him after five tries—he had yet to be first to circumnavigate the globe solo in a hot-air balloon. Fossett crossed that goal off his list in July, and now he can relax at last, his travels behind him, his feet up … yeah, right.

ROB GRIFFITH—AP/WIDE WORLD

Norah Jones
Singer

She was born to defy boundaries: Norah Jones grew up in Dallas, but she is sitar master Ravi Shankar's daughter. Her music, she claimed, "wasn't exactly jazz," yet her debut album, *Come Away with Me,* was released on one of jazz's most hallowed labels, Blue Note. On it, she performs both Hoagy Carmichael and Hank Williams. She sings with a poise you would expect from a veteran artist, but she is only 22. Straining to put a label on her soft-sell way with a song, critics compared her with not only Billie Holiday, Dinah Washington and Sarah Vaughan but also Willie Nelson, Aretha Franklin and Carole King. Jones was signed to Blue Note after a music exec heard the Texas college dropout sing in a New York City bar. She plays fame as coolly as she sings: not close with her father (she was born following a liaison between Shankar and a fan) she has refused to trade on his fame. "Buzz is cool," she told TIME. "Hype is not." Norah is cool.

GAVIN BOND—CORBIS OUTLINE

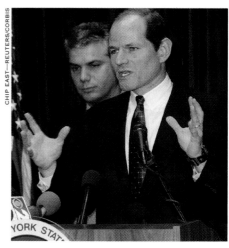

CHIP EAST—REUTERS/CORBIS

Eliot Spitzer
Crimebuster

When Eliot Spitzer limped into office as New York State's attorney general in 1998, he was an unlikely populist crusader. Having finished dead last in the Democratic primary in the previous election, Spitzer made it to the finish line on his second try by spending a sizable chunk of his father's real estate fortune. But in 2002 the wiry 43-year-old Harvard Law School graduate developed a national reputation as a giant slayer. Already known for taking up causes far removed from the usual concerns of a state attorney general—battling coal-burning power companies over acid rain, gunmakers over product liability, grocers for exploiting immigrant workers—Spitzer led a highly visible campaign in 2002 against abuses by some of America's biggest financial firms.

The "sheriff of Wall Street" focused first on Merrill Lynch, charging that the investment bank's analysts were routinely touting stocks of companies they knew were slumping. Merrill Lynch agreed to pay $100 million to settle the charges, and soon other brokerage houses were eager to meet with Spitzer—before he called on them. In the fall, Spitzer took on Citigroup, investigating charges that the financial giant showered lucrative initial public offerings of stock on CEOs who sent investment-banking business to Citi and devised complex financial schemes to help Enron conceal its debt.

Spitzer's critics—and there are many of them—contend that his crusades are all about political ambition. Their target is unfazed. "I'd rather have them say I'm opportunistic than wrong," Spitzer said.

V ERBATIM

Words wise—and otherwise

"You will be glad to know the President is practicing safe snacks."

Laura Bush, showing Jay Leno the pretzel that caused the President to choke and faint while watching TV

"It would be a mistake for the U.S. Senate to allow any kind of human cloning to come out of that chamber."

George W. Bush, on legislation banning cloning

"We've tripled the amount of money ... I believe it's from $50 million up to $195 million available."

George W. Bush, discussing U.S. aid, in Lima, Peru

"I understand that the unrest in the Middle East creates unrest throughout the region."

George W. Bush, on the Israeli-Palestinian conflict

"And so, in my State of the —my State of the Union —or State—my speech to the nation, whatever you want to call it, speech to the nation—I asked Americans to give 4,000 years—4,000 hours over the next—the rest of your life—of service to America. That's what I asked—4,000 hours."

George W. Bush, recapping his annual address

"Bush is not a moron at all; he's a friend."

Jean Chrétien, Canadian Prime Minister, on reports that his chief spokesman called the U.S. President a moron

"Not to idolize myself or anything like that, but I'm a big fan of me."

Jimmy Fallon, of *Saturday Night Live*

"My insecurities? I'm dumb, I'm stupid, I'm white, I'm ugly, I smell, I'm stupid, and I'm white."

Eminem

"She came, she stole, she left. End of story."

Ann Rundle, Los Angeles deputy district attorney, at Winona Ryder's shoplifting trial

"I made a terrible mistake. I got caught up in the excitement of the moment."

Michael Jackson, singer, explaining why he dangled his new son, Prince Michael II, over a balcony rail in Berlin

"My best pickup line is, 'I'm Hugh Hefner.' "

Hugh Hefner

"Everyone in Tinseltown is getting pinched, lifted and pulled. They lose some of their soul when they go under the knife."

Robert Redford, on Hollywood stars and cosmetic surgery

"He calls me Nana Newface. The kid has never seen me without a bandage."

Joan Rivers, on her grandson's reaction to her frequent surgeries

FREE WINONA

"I guess as long as people keep saying I have had plastic surgery, I can continue to put it off for a few more years."

Michelle Pfeiffer

"If I'd had as much plastic surgery as people say, there'd be another whole person left over! I could send her out to work *her* butt off onstage every night."

Cher

TERRORS & ERRORS

"From a marketing point of view, you don't introduce new products in August."

Andrew Card, White House chief of staff, on why he waited until September to launch the White House campaign to convince Americans that military action against Iraq is necessary

"Democracies die behind closed doors."

Sixth Circuit Court of Appeals, ruling that the Bush Administration must open deportation hearings of 9/11 suspects to the press and public

"How come I'm canceled, and bin Laden is still on al-Jazeera?"

Bill Maher, in a monologue on the last telecast of his defunct ABC talk show, *Politically Incorrect*

ALL MIXED UP

"I miss my sons, but there was nothing to eat."

Akhtar Muhammad, Afghan father, who sold two of his sons for bags of wheat

"In the days of slavery, there were those slaves who lived on the plantation and there were those slaves that lived in the house … When Colin Powell dares to suggest something other than what the master wants to hear, he will be turned back out to pasture."

Harry Belafonte, on San Diego radio station KFMB

"If Harry had wanted to attack my politics, that was fine … But to use a slave reference, I think, is unfortunate."

Colin Powell, in response

"He barks a lot. But he's useless."

Two Israeli soldiers, on why they named a stray dog George W. Bush

"This proves he is the finest athlete in the world."

Rich Shea, spokesman, on world hot-dog-eating champion Takeru Kobayashi, who defended his title by eating 50.5 dogs in 12 min.

"We sell seats, and if you consume more than one seat, you have to buy more than one seat."

Beth Harbin, a Southwest Airlines spokeswoman, defending a policy to charge large passengers for two seats

BAD COMPANY

"I want to focus on my salad."

Martha Stewart, avoiding questions about the ImClone scandal on CBS's *The Early Show*

"It would be unthinkable to deprive people of my expertise."

Harvey Pitt, embattled SEC head, defending his ability to run an agency overseeing companies that were once his clients

"Enron robbed the bank, Arthur Andersen provided the getaway car, and they say you were at the wheel."

Representative Jim Greenwood, to fired Andersen auditor David Duncan

"Such a piece of crap."

Private e-mail from a **Merrill Lynch analyst,** referring to the stock of Excite@home; publicly, Merrill Lynch gave it a "buy" recommendation

Nation

Parched: A Doozy of A Drought Makes for A Long, Hot Summer

For many Americans—like Bob Roberts, a farmer in Scottsbluff, Neb.—the summer of '02 will be recalled as a time of drought, even if a series of spectacular wildfires got more attention. The drought was a double-header, with one huge tentacle of hot, dry air covering 14 Western states from Montana to Arizona and another mighty arm frying 14 states along the Eastern seaboard. Result: clambakes and rodeos canceled, lawns and pastures blistered—only the grasshoppers liked it. Cautious scientists refused to call the long dry spell global warming. Americans called it all kinds of things, most of them unprintable here.

RIGHT TURN

George Bush leads the Republican Party to a historic victory in
the midterm elections, and the G.O.P. takes control of Congress

GEORGE BUSH WAS SO CONFIDENT OF THE RESULTS OF the November midterm elections that he threw an election-night party in the White House's family dining room. The get-together was officially billed as a celebration of George and Laura Bush's 25th wedding anniversary, but the gifts had barely been presented and the roast beef eaten before a television set was wheeled in for the President and his guests to watch the returns.

They made for pleasant viewing. Just after dessert was served, an aide handed Bush the phone: his father was calling from Florida to tell him that Bush's brother Jeb was running well in the Governor's race. Soon the results of several of the close Senate races started to arrive, and Bush began to place congratulatory phone calls to Republican candidates all around the country, including John Sununu

ON THE STUMP: Barnstorming around the nation before the election, George Bush rallies the faithful in Knoxville, Tenn.

in New Hampshire and Elizabeth Dole in North Carolina.

The next morning the White House dispatched an e-mail to Republican leaders with the day's official line: "No gloating." Bush's team had won the biggest presidential triumph in a midterm election in nearly a century—and had recaptured control of the Senate, lost by the G.O.P. in May 2001, when Vermont Senator Jim Jeffords left the party to become an independent who usually voted with the Democrats. While the overall G.O.P. victory margin was small, the party prevailed in most of its high-priority races. In Georgia, Saxby Chambliss coasted to an upset win over incumbent Senator Max Cleland. In Minnesota, where the race had been thrown into turmoil by the tragic death of incumbent Democrat Senator Paul Wellstone only days before the election, Republican Norm Coleman defeated the hurriedly drafted former Vice President, Walter Mondale. In Missouri, Bush's hand-picked candidate, former Congressman Jim Talent, defeated Senator Jean Carnahan, elected in 2000 when her husband, the sitting Governor, was killed in a plane crash shortly before the voting.

Bush earned his celebration: the nation's right turn followed the President's active campaigning around the country in the weeks before voters went to the polls. The idea of sending Bush himself out into the midterm storms wasn't a last-minute decision; it was made early in the year by Bush's political adviser of the past 15 years, Karl Rove. In the final weeks of battle, it was Rove's ability to deliver the President, and Bush's to deliver the voters, that seemed to have turned the tide.

By the eve of the election, G.O.P. polls projected a big turnout by Republican voters energized by Bush's full-court press: he visited 15 states in the last five days before the election. Democratic strategists, meanwhile, underestimated his pull. Said Democrat operative Tony Coelho, chairman of Al Gore's 2000 campaign: "What they did was risky as hell. They rolled the dice, they won, and now Bush has a huge mandate. It's not about 9/11 anymore. He is the legitimate President."

Indeed, 21 out of the 23 House candidates and 12 of the 16 Senate candidates Bush campaigned for won their races. Only three other times in the past century had a President's party gained seats in the House in an off-year election, and not since the Civil War had the President's party won back a Senate majority in a midterm contest. Bush will be the first G.O.P. President since Dwight Eisenhower to enjoy outright majorities in the House and Senate.

One unplanned event also played into the Republicans' hands: Democrats turned an Oct. 29 memorial service for Minnesota's Senator Wellstone into a pep rally, booing G.O.P. Senate leader Trent Lott, who had come to pay his respects. The ensuing backlash against the politically charged event almost certainly helped Coleman beat out Mondale for Wellstone's Senate seat. A private poll by Bill Clinton's former pollster, Mark Penn, suggest-

ed that the service backfired on the Democrats nationally as well. Penn found that 68% of voters knew about the service—a high awareness of an event broadcast live nationally only on C-SPAN. What's more, 49% of voters said the service made them less likely to vote for a Democrat—and 67% of independents said they felt that way.

Penn's poll also pinpointed the issue that loomed even larger in the election: homeland security. A stunning 65% of voters surveyed thought Democrats weren't supportive enough of the President's war on terror. Once Bush hit the campaign trail, Republican candidates played up their advantages on national-security issues to voters nervous about terrorism and Iraq. Democrats tried to focus on the economy, but the party never settled on an alternative to Bush's policies of big tax cuts and increased defense spending. "The most important thing was the message that we were trying to articulate," said Democratic Senator Harry Reid of Nevada, the top deputy to sitting majority leader Tom Daschle of South Dakota. "It did not go anyplace. People were more interested in Sept. 11, the [Washington, D.C.-area] sniper and the Iraq war."

The Republicans' greatest victory was their takeover of the Senate. At 2 a.m. on election night, shortly after Carnahan conceded defeat in Missouri, an aide to Trent Lott sneaked into his empty Capitol office and placed a bronze plaque engraved with the words MAJORITY LEADER on Lott's desk. The plaque had been stowed in the bottom drawer of the desk since Jeffords' defection, but Lott never threw it away, just in case he returned to the Senate's top job. "I just feel exhilarated about having another opportunity," he told TIME.

He got a chance to show his new muscle when Congress convened in a lame-duck session after the election. The Senate quickly passed legislation authorizing a new federal Department of Homeland Security—a bill that had been delayed for months by partisan disputes. Now in full control of Congress, the Administration will be expected to produce more such results. But like President Eisenhower's before him, George Bush's popularity seems to rest heavily on his prestige as Commander in Chief rather than on deep support for his domestic policies. The results will be interesting. ∎

Lott

Pelosi and Gephardt

DAVE MARTIN—AP/WIDE WORLD; KENNETH LAMBERT—AP/WIDE WORLD

A CHANGE OF GUARD ON THE HILL

Just as Republican Trent Lott of Mississippi was preparing to resume his former post as Senate Majority Leader, he got himself into hot water with an off-the-cuff remark at the 100th birthday party of retiring South Carolina Senator Strom Thurmond. Said Lott, "I want to say this about my state: When Strom Thurmond ran for president, we voted for him. We're proud of it. And if the rest of the country had followed our lead, we wouldn't have had all these problems over all these years, either." (Thurmond split the Democratic Party to run on a pro-segregation platform in 1948.) When Lott was berated for his words, he began issuing a series of increasingly labored apologies. Finally even the White House said it would not support him, and the chances that he would survive as Majority Leader in 2003 seemed very slim.

In the House, longtime Democratic leader Richard Gephardt of Missouri resigned his post after the midterm defeat. The party's new leader: **former whip Nancy Pelosi of San Francisco, an unapologetic liberal. Representative Tom DeLay, a hard-right Texan, will be the House majority leader, taking the position of fellow Texan Dick Armey, who retired.**

WHY THE SENATE IS NOW BACK IN G.O.P. HANDS

Credit Democratic apathy and a hustling campaigner-in-chief

SENATE RESULTS

Republican   Democrat   No election

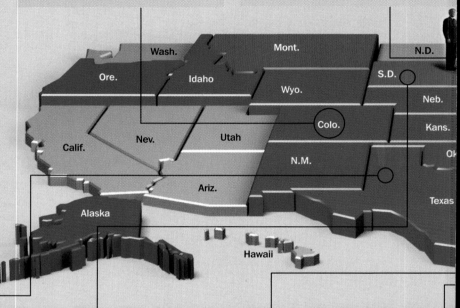

FIVE DAYS, 15 STATES
Cities in which Bush campaigned five days before the election

CHRISTOPHER MORRIS—VII

COLORADO

Wayne Allard

The veterinarian beat '96 loser Tom Strickland in a bitter rematch. Their nasty tone drove loyal partisans to the polls but kept independents home. It hurt Strickland—Republicans outnumber Democrats in this state

The key to victory
Allard won the **southern Denver suburbs** and rural areas

MINNESOTA

Norm Coleman

After Paul Wellstone's death, Coleman, 53, hit the perfect tone in ads—respectful but looking toward the future. With Mondale, 74, and gubernatorial candidate Roger Moe, 61, on their ticket, the Democrats looked like the past

The key to victory
The partisan **memorial service** for Wellstone turned off independents

ED ANDREISKI—AP/WIDE WORLD

TEXAS
Republican attorney general John Cornyn defeated Ron Kirk despite the Dallas mayor's moderate record

SOUTH DAKOTA
Tom Daschle's fellow Democrat Tim Johnson beat Congressman John Thune by just 528 votes

ARKANSAS
Mark Pryor defeated Republican Senator Tim Hutchinson in the Democrats' only pickup of the night

LOUISIANA
Mary Landrieu successfully defended her seat against Republican Suzanne Haik Terrell in a December runoff

Sources: AP, *The Cook Political Report*, National Governors Association

REPUBLICANS HOLD THE HOUSE ...

Just 16 of 435 seats were truly up for grabs this election, and Democrats won only five. Here were some of the key battles:

HOUSE RESULTS

Republicans	**229**	(Gain of 5)
Democrats	**204**	(Loss of 7)
Independent	**1**	Undecided as of 12/1C

ALABAMA
3rd District
G.O.P. wins 50.4%-48.2%

Democrat Joe Turnham challenged Republican Mike Rogers to a skeet-shooting contest to prove he wasn't a liberal. It didn't work

NEW YORK
1st District
Democrats win 50.1%-48.6%

Absentee ballots are still being counted, but college provost Tim Bishop won a surprise upset against first-term Republican Felix Grucci

COLORADO
7th District
G.O.P. wins 47.4%-47.2%

Republican Bob Beauprez finally claimed victory over Democrat Mike Feeley on Dec.11, after provisional ballots were counted

KENTUCKY
3rd District
G.O.P. wins 51.6%-48.4%

Incumbent Anne Northup got a break and challenger Jack Conway took a hit when his boss, the Governor, was hit with a sex scandal

FLORIDA
5th District
G.O.P. wins 47.9%-46.3%

Half of this redrawn district's voters were new to Democratic Representative Karen Thurman, giving Ginny Brown-Waite an upset

MISSOURI

Jim Talent

Two years after being appointed to succeed her late husband, Jean Carnahan lost to Talent, who made an issue of who would be more loyal to the President as he continues the war on terrorism. Talent won—by just 1% of the 1,867,432 votes

The key to victory
Republicans attacked Carnahan for not voting to make the **tax cuts** permanent

GEORGIA

Saxby Chambliss

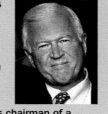

In a big upset, Chambliss beat Max Cleland. Republican ads accused the Democrat, a Vietnam vet and triple amputee, of being soft on national security. Chambliss is chairman of a subcommittee on terrorism

The key to victory
President Bush **visited three times** and told voters Chambliss would be his ally

NEW HAMPSHIRE

John E. Sununu

Democrat Jeanne Shaheen built a reputation as a moderate during three terms as Governor and outspent Sununu by $1.3 million. But he successfully painted her as a tax-and-spend liberal—dirty words in this state

The key to victory
Shaheen was able to attract only 4% of **independent** voters

Wis.
Mich.
Ill.
Mo.
Ind.
Ohio
Ky.
Tenn.
Ark.
Miss.
Ala.
La.
S.C.
Ga.
N.C.
Va.
W.Va.
Pa.
N.Y.
Vt.
N.H.
Maine
Mass.
R.I.
Conn.
N.J.
Del.
Md.
Fla.

Republicans **51**
(Gain of 2)

34 seats up
for election

Democrats **48**
(Loss of 2)

Independent **1**

TENNESSEE

Former Education Secretary Lamar Alexander won the fight to keep Fred Thompson's seat in the Republican column

SOUTH CAROLINA

Republican Representative Lindsey Graham won retiring Strom Thurmond's seat. Will Graham serve 50 years too?

NORTH CAROLINA

Despite a shrinking lead just before the vote, Elizabeth Dole held on to beat Clinton chief of staff Erskine Bowles

NEW JERSEY

After two years off, Frank Lautenberg,78, is back on Capitol Hill after stepping in for Bob Torricelli

... WHILE DEMOCRATS GAIN GOVERNORS

Republican

No election; Republican

Democrat

No election; Democrat

With G.O.P. incumbents stepping down, Democrats had a shot at gaining up to seven seats. But with Bush fueling turnout, they picked up just three. Georgia got its first Republican Governor since Reconstruction

Text By Mitch Frank

WAGING WAR ON TERRORISM

Since the deadly attacks of Sept. 11, 2001, Americans have battled a new enemy: stateless, suicidal terrorists. The conflict took place on many fronts. Abroad, U.S. soldiers remained in Afghanistan to ensure the peace, even as bombs exploded in Bali and Kenya. At home, the government created a vast new federal agency, the Department of Homeland Security, charged with fighting terror. In the courts, trials of suspected terrorists were under way. In the airports, new security teams checked baggage and flyers. Even so, al-Qaeda and its allies were at large and active, armed and dangerous.

AT HOME

■ HOMELAND SECURITY

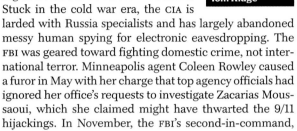

Tom Ridge

In the wake of 9/11, the CIA and FBI were intensely criticized for not having detected and thwarted the attacks. Stuck in the cold war era, the CIA is larded with Russia specialists and has largely abandoned messy human spying for electronic eavesdropping. The FBI was geared toward fighting domestic crime, not international terror. Minneapolis agent Coleen Rowley caused a furor in May with her charge that top agency officials had ignored her office's requests to investigate Zacarias Moussaoui, which she claimed might have thwarted the 9/11 hijackings. In November, the FBI's second-in-command, Bruce Gebhardt, fired off a memo saying that some super-

Robert Mueller   George Tenet

visors in agency field offices still lacked a "sense of urgency" in hunting terrorists.

Both CIA Director George Tenet and FBI boss Robert Mueller were intensely grilled by congressional committees but held onto their jobs. Still, George Bush created a presidential commission to study the attacks in late November. He asked Henry Kissinger, 79, to lead it, but the former Secretary of State soon withdrew, citing possible conflicts of interest with his famously secret client list.

In June, President Bush (who had initially opposed the idea) proposed creating a new Department of Homeland Security, which in theory would help the U.S. fight terror by consolidating many formerly scattered agencies under one centralized authority. Partisan disputes over employee rights hung up the bill for months, but it passed in the November lame-duck congressional session. Bush named Tom Ridge, the former Pennsylvania Governor who had led the White House homeland security team since the 9/11 attacks, to head up the new agency.

More than 85% of the 170,000 people assigned to the new department will be involved in controlling the nation's borders, duties previously performed by the Coast Guard (Transportation), Customs (Treasury), and Immigration and Naturalization (Justice). The sprawling department will also create a nationwide communications system to speed information sharing. It is the largest shuffling of the federal bureaucracy since Harry Truman combined War and Navy into a single Defense Department after World War II, and it may be years, experts said, before it is running smoothly.

■ AIRPORT SECURITY

One year after Congress created a new Transportation Security Administration (TSA) and ordered it to replace the private-sector baggage screeners who had been providing lax check-in security at airports, the new agency had hired, trained and deployed more than 40,000 professional baggage screeners to the nation's 400-plus airports. Early on, the new screeners earned high marks for being polite, thorough and efficient.

But the TSA also faced a second, more difficult deadline: a congressional mandate to install automated explosives-detection equipment in all major U.S. airports by Dec. 31. (Officials were cautiously optimistic about meeting this date.) The TSA is also developing a "trusted traveler" program, under which U.S. citizens who agree to submit to a background check will be issued credentials that allow them to move through security checkpoints much faster than usual. In addition, the agency is designing a computerized passenger-profiling system that will red-flag potential security threats.

The TSA will also train airline pilots to use firearms and equip cockpits with guns, as required by a law passed by Congress in September (pilots and the public were in favor; the Bush Administration and the airlines opposed it). Funding for the program has not yet passed, so only a few pilots will be armed in the the near term. Far less publicity has attended the federal air marshals program, which had fewer than 50 employees on Sept. 11, 2001. There are now more than 1,000 marshals flying undercover aboard U.S. carriers (the exact number is secret), and their ranks are expected to top 6,000 within a few years.

GRIN AND BEAR IT: Passengers clog up the security checkpoints at the Denver airport in May

AFGHANISTAN: 101st Airborne troops scramble out of a Chinook helicopter in March, one day after seven U.S. soldiers died in battle

AROUND THE WORLD

■ WHERE IS OSAMA BIN LADEN?

The mastermind behind the international terror organization al-Qaeda was last heard from, U.S. officials said, in early December 2001, when his voice was intercepted directing his warriors by radio as U.S. airplanes bombed their redoubts in the Tora Bora region of eastern Afghanistan. But bin Laden slipped away, and for 10 months was neither seen nor heard from, leading many to suspect—or hope—that he was dead. Then in mid-November, the al-Jazeera TV station in Qatar broadcast an audiotape it claimed was made by bin Laden. The tape cited several recent terrorist attacks, and U.S. authorities said they thought it was authentic.

The tape was an unhappy reminder that the U.S. had failed in the primary objective of its antiterrorism war, the apprehension of bin Laden and the breakup of al-Qaeda. George Bush had declared soon after 9/11 that he wanted bin Laden "dead or alive"—then had refused to even utter the terrorist's name when the U.S. conspicuously did not get its man.

Osama bin Laden

Where is bin Laden? Most analysts believed he was holed up in Pakistan's remote border zone, or perhaps he was hidden by sympathizers in dusty Peshawar, the chief city of Pakistan's remote Northwest Frontier. His No. 2 man, the Egyptian Ayman al-Zawahiri, was also believed to be alive.

The good news: the U.S. apprehended three top al-Qaeda operatives in 2002. Abu Zubaydah, 31, a Saudiborn Palestinian who helped assemble the inner mechanisms of al-Qaeda, was captured in April in Faisalabad,

Abu Zubayadh

Pakistan, along with a trove of information. Ramzi Binalshibh, 30, a Yemeni who helped plan the 9/11 hijackings, was captured in Karachi, Pakistan, in September. In November Abd al-Rahim al-Nashiri, a thirtyish Saudi who is suspected of planning the attack on the U.S.S. *Cole* in 2000 and the 1998 East African embassy bombings, was nabbed; U.S. officials would not say where. And in one of the most pro-active strikes to date in the U.S. war on terror, senior al-Qaeda leader Qaed Salim Sinan al-Harethi and five others were incinerated by a missile fired by a CIA-operated Predator drone in Yemen on November 2.

■ THE WAR IN AFGHANISTAN

Though the U.S. toppled Afghanistan's Islamist Taliban regime late in 2001, some 8,000 U.S. troops (and an undisclosed number of allied soldiers) remained on the ground in 2002. Their mission: keep the peace, support the fledgling government of new President Hamid Karzai, continue to search out and destroy Taliban and al-Qaeda elements. The year's largest engagement was Operation Anaconda in March. Some 1,000 U.S. troops were airlifted into the Shah-i-Kot region south of Kabul to rout al-Qaeda fighters, but they ran into more opposition than they expected;

eight Americans were killed in the fighting. Still, U.S. military officials called the operation a success, saying hundreds of al-Qaeda operatives or sympathizers were killed.

Karzai's presidency, formalized in June, was tested when a car bomb exploded in Kabul on Sept. 5, killing 32 people. A few hours later, an al-Qaeda agent tried to kill Karzai in Kandahar; U.S. troops guarding Karzai killed him. But America lost much goodwill among Afghans when U.S. bombs wiped out an innocent wedding party and twice hit gatherings of Karzai allies. The U.S. is eager to hand off peacekeeping duties in the nation to the 5,000-person International Security Assistance Force, but American personnel may remain in Afghanistan for years.

■ A NEW ROUND OF ATTACKS

After a year on the run, al-Qaeda and its allies launched a series of attacks in October that amounted to a new offensive. On Oct. 2, an explosion in a karaoke bar in the Philippines killed three people, including a U.S. Green Beret. On Oct. 6, the French oil tanker *Limburg* was rammed by an explosives-laden boat off the coast of Yemen; one crew member died, and 90,000 barrels of oil leaked into the Gulf of Aden. On the 8th, two Kuwaitis attacked U.S. Marines at a training facility, killing one of them.

Then, on Oct. 12, terrorists launched a massive strike on Indonesia's resort island of Bali. Three synchronized bombs exploded outside a nightclub, killing more than 190 people, most of them foreign tourists from Australia. The Bali bombing is believed to have been the work of Jemaah Islamiah, a local terror group closely linked to al-Qaeda.

On Nov. 28, suicide bombers set off a blast at the Paradise Hotel outside Mombasa, Kenya, a favorite of Israeli tourists. Ten Kenyans and three Israelis were killed; scores were injured. At almost the same time, two shoulder-launched heat-seeking missiles were fired at a charter jet carrying 271 Israelis as it took off from the Mombasa airport, but both missed. U.S. intelligence officials said the attacks were very likely the work of al-Qaeda. ■

BALI: The bombs gave notice that the war on terror was a global conflict

RAKADEN—RADAR—REUTERS—LANDOV

IN THE COURTS

SHANE T. MCCOY—U.S. NAVY—AP/WIDE WORLD

DETAINED: Prisoners are held at Camp X Ray in Cuba

It's an enduring American issue: How to balance domestic security with civil liberties? In November the U.S. Foreign Intelligence Surveillance Court of Review overturned a decision by a lower court that had denied the Justice Department the broad surveillance and intelligence-sharing powers granted under the Patriot Act of 2001. Civil libertarians were also alarmed when the legislation setting up the Department of Homeland Security widened federal authority to monitor Internet traffic.

In other legal issues surrounding the war on terrorism:

John Walker Lindh

Z. Moussaoui

Richard Reid

■ John Walker Lindh, 21, an American captured in 2001 while fighting alongside Taliban troops in Afghanistan, pleaded guilty in July to two counts of aiding the Taliban and carrying explosives. He was sentenced to 20 years in prison.
■ Zacarias Moussaoui, 34, the French citizen accused of conspiring to take part in the 9/11 attacks, is now slated to be tried on June 30, 2003. The trial date was moved back twice in 2002 by a federal court in Alexandria, Va.
■ Richard Reid, 29, a British citizen, pleaded guilty in October to eight charges surrounding his attempt to set off explosives in his shoe aboard a Paris-to-Miami flight late in 2001. He will be sentenced in January 2003.
■ As of Dec. 1, 2002, more than 600 foreign detainees were being held by the U.S. in Guantánamo Bay, Cuba. Four men were let go in October, the first to be freed. The camp has been criticized because inmates are held without charges and are not allowed access to lawyers.

A Time To Remember

Americans pause to reflect on the
horrors—and heroism—of 9/11/01

For Americans, 2002 was the year after—
a year of reaction, a year lived in an echo
chamber, a year whose identity was
shaped not by its own events but by the
momentous terrorist attacks of Sept. 11,
2001. Many challenges posed by that day's events
were still unresolved. Though the Taliban regime
had been toppled, American troops were still
fighting in Afghanistan, and the masterminds behind the 9/11 attacks were still at large.

Yet Americans looked back at the horrors of
2001 not only in anger but also with sorrow and
pride. The sorrow recalled the frightening murder
of so many innocent civilians and the horrible
manner of their deaths. But the pride was perhaps
even more important, for Americans had responded
with courage, sacrifice and dignity to the stern
challenges of that morning. Sixteen acres in lower
Manhattan and a field in rural Pennsylvania were
now hallowed ground, consecrated to the memory
of heroes who died there while helping others. At
a ceremony honoring those who perished at the
Pentagon, Secretary of Defense Donald Rumsfeld
spoke for many when he said, "The terrorists
wanted Sept. 11 to be a day when innocents died.
Instead it was a day when heroes were born." ■

FIELD OF HONOR
Susan and Pat Halloran, with daughter
Claire, attend the memorial service for
victims of United Airlines Flight 93 near
Shanksville, Pa., on 9/11/02. President
Bush visited the crash site later in the
day. Claire Halloran was an intern at the
White House on 9/11/01.

10/11/01

JUSTIN SULLIVAN—GETTY IMAGES

SPENCER PLATT—GETTY IMAGES

FROM THE ASHES

This sequence of pictures shows the rapid progress of the enormous cleanup job at ground zero. The work continued 24 hours a day, seven days a week, for 261 days; required 3.1 million man-hours of labor; and moved some 1,642,698 tons of material. The job finished ahead of schedule, and the cost—$750 million—was far below initial estimates of $7 billion.

ELKIN YUEN

1/18/02

8/27/02

WITH BOWED HEAD

At left, a police officer mourns the victims at the anniversary memorial ceremony at ground zero. The New York City police department lost 23 officers that day; the New York City fire department lost 343 fire fighters.

OVERWHELMED

Dwarfed by the enormous retaining wall, or "bathtub," that once held the foundations of the Twin Towers of the World Trade Center, family members of victims form a circle at the bottom of the pit. Six preliminary plans to rebuild the site were presented to the public in the summer and met with substantial criticism; opponents charged that the plans called for too much office space at the expense of a memorial to the tragedy's victims.

WE WILL NEVER FORGET

CORBIS SYGMA

MAKESHIFT MEMORIAL
A man leaves a photograph on a memorial circle of remembrances at ground zero at the anniversary service. During the ceremony, the names of the victims of the 9/11 attack were read in order; former New York City Mayor Rudolph Giuliani was the first reader. One heartening surprise: in November 2002 two individuals who were thought to have died in New York City—and whose names were read that morning—were found to be alive, bringing the current death toll for the Manhattan attack to 2,795.

HAIL FROM THE CHIEF
Left, President Bush and Secretary of Defense Donald Rumsfeld join 13,000 other Americans in reciting the Pledge of Allegiance during the anniversary service at the Pentagon, where 189 people died on 9/11. The building was completely restored ahead of schedule, a month before the ceremony; the restoration of the limestone façade is so thorough that some visitors to the building have to inquire where the jet struck.

CLUES ON ICE

Below, frozen vials of DNA samples await a match. By the first anniversary of the attacks, 648 of the 2,795 victims had been identified through DNA alone. The New York City medical examiner's office hopes to identify at least 2,000 victims by the spring of 2003.

RICHARD PRESS

TOM HANSON—AP/WIDE WORLD

A HERO REMEMBERED

Above, two members of the family of New York City fire fighter Paul John Gill burst into tears as his name is read during the memorial ceremony at ground zero. Earlier, New York City Mayor Michael Bloomberg led the city in a moment of silence at 8:46 a.m., when the North Tower was struck. After attending the Pentagon service, President Bush visited both the Pennsylvania site and ground zero, then addressed the nation from Ellis Island in the evening.

SOLEMN CONCLUSION

Two memorial services were held at ground zero in 2002. At left, on May 30, during a ceremony that officially ended the cleanup and recovery efforts, New York City police officers and Red Cross workers salute as an empty flag-draped stretcher—symbolizing victims not recovered—is removed from the disaster site. The May 30 service began at 10:29 a.m., the time that the second of the two World Trade Center towers collapsed on 9/11.

SUZANNE PLUNKETT—AP/WIDE WORLD

SAVED!

Buried alive, nine coal miners are unearthed by a skillful team of rescuers

TRAPPED 24 STORIES UNDERGROUND, NINE PENNSYL-vania coal miners huddle back to back for warmth. Cold, hungry and wet, they wait for help in absolute darkness, with floodwaters lapping at their feet. A 5-in.-wide pipe hurriedly rammed into the ground by frantic rescuers above is their lifeline, feeding them warm compressed air—air whose pressure helps stave off the floodwaters lapping at their feet. A cord binds them together. But there are other ties that bind them: they pray together, speak quietly of their families and scrawl their last thoughts to their wives and children. High above them, over the course of three long days, rescue officials downplay hopes for their survival.

Then, early on a Sunday morning, after 77 nerve-racking hours, the first of the miners emerges from the ground, and the eight others quickly follow. Their rescue is a dramatic story of human resolve and resourcefulness, and it is best told just as it unfolded.

Wednesday, July 24, 9 p.m. The Quecreek mine lies about 55 miles southeast of Pittsburgh, only 10 miles from Shanksville, where hijacked United Airlines Flight 93 crashed on 9/11/01. Within the mine, 240 ft. beneath the soil, a nine-man team of miners is nearing the end of a shift. Mark (Moe) Popernack, the crew's operator, is cutting into a seam of coal when he unexpectedly breaks through into the adjacent Saxman mine, abandoned for 50 years and completely flooded with water. The crew's incorrect maps showed its tunnels to be 300 ft. away.

Flood! A wall of water 4 ft. high explodes through the fissure, and the miners scramble to outrun it. Dennis (Harpo) Hall, 49, telephones a warning to a second crew working nearby: "We've got major water!" The other team manages to escape the quickly rising waters. But the nine are not so lucky; after hours of searching for exits, they battle upstream against the flood and take refuge in the highest cavern they can find, knowing that the 20-ft. by 40-ft. space holds a limited supply of oxygen—and wait to be rescued.

Thursday, July 25, 1 a.m. Within hours of the accident, a massive response team has assembled: federal, state and local officials, mining experts, medical personnel—some 300 people in all. The emergency team, guessing that the men, if alive, have headed for high ground, sink a 5-in. pipe into the earth, through which they feed compressed hot air. It is a brilliant piece of guesswork. Incredibly, the pipe emerges near the relieved miners, who reply in the age-old code of those who delve in the earth: they strike the pipe nine times, a signal that nine men are alive below. The clanging sends a shock of jubilation and hope through the gaggle of workers and miners' relatives gathered above.

But the situation belowground is getting worse. The nine men tie themselves together with a metal cord looped through their belts. They agree to survive—or not survive—as a unit. Much of their ordeal is spent in complete darkness; they decide to save their two working headlights in case they are needed during the rescue. They find a lunchbox floating by and open it to find a single sandwich and two sodas, which they share. But they are out of snuff, and a miner without his "chew" is not a happy miner.

Thursday, July 25, 2:30 p.m. Workers on the surface cheer when a large drill rig finally rolls in, trucked from a West Virginia mine. It takes several hours to

RELIEF: No, they're not going to Disney World—but the happy miners signed a deal for their story with the Walt Disney Co.

assemble the machine, but by 6 p.m. it roars into life—and the miners below take hope: they can hear the drill bit chewing its way through the ground.

Eight hours later, the hum of the drill suddenly stops: 100 ft. down, the 1,500-lb. bit has broken, and the rescue effort is stalled. The sudden silence, the miners later said, was perhaps the lowest point of their ordeal. As the quiet hours pass in the dark, they share a single pen to write farewell notes on scraps of cardboard they have found and seal the notes in a lunch pail for safe-keeping.

Friday, July 26, 11:10 a.m. Working with new equipment, the rescue team begins drilling a second shaft, 75 ft. from the first (it will reach 204 ft. down before a broken pipe halts it). Wells have also been drilled into the mine, and water is being removed by dozens of pumps at a rate of 20,000 gal. a minute. Rescue workers later suspect that the 18-hr. delay caused by the broken drill bit was providential; if the drill had broken into the miners' air pocket before most of the water was pumped out, the area would probably have been flooded. At 4:45 p.m., the broken bit is removed from the first shaft, where work resumes some three hours later. But it will take more than 24 hours of solid drilling before the shaft reaches the men.

Saturday, July 27, 10:16 p.m. The drill breaks through into the cavern. Rescue worker Rob Zaremski lowers a microphone into the shaft, waits—then turns and gives a thumbs-up to the crowd. A moment later, he flashes nine fingers to indicate the men are all safe. A telephone is lowered, and the miners are asked, "Anybody there?" The reply is, "Yes. What took you so long?" Two hours later, when the slim, 7-ft.-tall yellow rescue cylinder reaches the men, it is filled with blankets, jackets, water—and snuff.

Sunday, July 28, 1 a.m. Crew chief Randy Fogle is the first miner to reach the surface, where he is greeted with a huge roar from the crowd. Within two hours, all the miners have been rescued. They are taken to two hospitals, where doctors say they are in excellent shape, given their ordeal. None of them suffer lasting effects. Several of the miners speak of their astonishment at the size of the rescue effort that was mounted on their behalf. And for those who were wondering, says Fogle, "I don't believe too many of us will go back to that kind of work." ■

WORRIED: Above, a rescue worker strains to hear signs of life beneath, while two women anxiously await good news

BEHIND THE KILLER SMILES

POSING AS FAMILY: Malvo, left, and Muhammad visit the older man's relatives in Baton Rouge, La., in July

A massive manhunt nabs two deadly snipers and halts a reign of fear

THE FIRST OF THE BULLETS THAT STRAFED THE SUBURBS of Washington D.C. in the fall of 2002 sliced through the air over a drab strip-mall parking lot in Aspen Hill, Md., on Oct. 2 and cracked a nickel-size hole in the front window of a Michaels craft store, then fell to the floor. Unlike every shot that followed over the next three weeks, the bullet hurt no one. But its fragments, lying on the store floor, stated the theme of the maddening, frightening siege that soon followed: no matter how upscale the neighborhood, no matter how comfortable the surroundings, you too could be a target. A malicious hunter—or hunters—had taken position in the natural habitat of contemporary Americans. Yet as one horrific killing succeeded another until 10 people were dead, no one saw the shooter: the anonymous, banal suburbs, it turns out, make a better shooting gallery than a dark alley.

Before the unlikely pair behind the killings were apprehended 22 days later, they conducted one of the most terrifying murder rampages in U.S. history. Almost every institution in the D.C. area was affected: homes and schools were locked up tight, workplaces were tense, parks and restaurants and shopping malls sat vacant and still. The snipers reigned over daily life, tied up traffic, dominated the news, controlled everyone's thoughts. The case elicited 138,000 tip-line phone calls, seven times the number the Unabomber case yielded over 18 years.

Because the crime scenes ringed the nation's capital, few resources were spared in the search for the killer. By the end of the first week, more than 1,000 people were working the case, including Bureau of Alcohol, Tobacco and Firearms (ATF) units, U.S. marshals and state police. How did the alleged snipers—John Allen Muhammad,

41, and his companion, Jamaican-born John Lee Malvo, only 17—elude one of the greatest dragnets in U.S. history? First, they were crafty. Muhammad, born John Allen Williams in Louisiana, took a new surname after joining the Nation of Islam in 1985. A Gulf War veteran and a trained Army marksman, he modified his car to make it a highly efficient killing machine. A hole cut in its trunk allowed for firing from a prone position in its rear—explaining why the sniper was never seen and almost no shell casings were found at the murder sites. Second, the authorities, acting on serial-killer profiles, focused their search on an angry white male, acting alone, while eyewitness accounts of a white truck or panel van at several of the murder scenes further misguided the police. Third, since the pair seemed to have no motive for murder, other than free-floating rage, they left no pattern to trace. There was no method in their madness.

The snipers' first bullet was followed in less than an hour by a second: James Martin was gunned down in a parking lot a little more than two miles from the first shooting. Not only did the killer brazenly fire during the rush-hour congestion period, but he also took aim right across the street from a police station. This first success seemed to launch the snipers on a bloody rampage: on the next morning, Oct. 3, they shot and killed four people in just over two hours. The day's fifth victim was gunned down later, at 9:20 p.m.

In this first—and by far the worst—outburst, the snipers killed six people in only 28 hours, most of whom were engaged in carrying out the routine tasks of everyday life. No pattern seemed to connect the murders. The victims were a random sampling of the Washington metropolitan area: they were white, black, Hispanic, Indian, male, female. There was a government analyst, a landscaper, a housekeeper, a nanny. Police had one clue: all the victims were shot by the same weapon, a .223-cal. rifle. And witnesses at one site said they saw a white truck flee the scene. The false trail would mislead police for weeks.

The first shootings were at least united by proximity. But on Oct. 4 the snipers struck again, this time in a parking lot in Spotsylvania County, Va., about 70 miles from the

FEAR: A parent walks his child from a Bowie, Md., middle school

other attacks. The victim, a woman shopping at a Michaels store, was injured but survived. By now, only a few days into the murder spree, the public had grown familiar with the man leading the manhunt: Charles Moose, 49, chief of police of Montgomery County, Md., site of the first shootings. In a televised briefing on Sunday, Oct. 6, Chief Moose expressed concern for local children and promised to "greatly increase" police presence at area schools the following day. The sniper seemed to have been listening: the next morning, an eighth-grade boy was shot in front of Benjamin Tasker Middle School in Bowie, Md. The boy, who survived, had just been dropped off by his aunt less than 20 ft. from the school door.

Even as Chief Moose was declaring of the murder rampage, "I guess it's getting to be really, really personal now," evidence at the latest crime scene was backing him up. Police found a tarot "death" card with the message "Mister Policeman, I am God." The card also contained a request not to tell the media about its existence. When reports of the card leaked, an angry Moose condemned both the press and the leaker. A dialogue between the murderers and their pursuers was developing, and the chief's credibility with his prey was paramount; by the end of the month, Moose seemed to be using his public appearances

THREE WEEKS OF FEAR

OCT. 2, 5:20 p.m. James D. Martin, 55, an environmental analyst for the U.S. government, is killed while walking across a parking lot in Wheaton, Md.

OCT. 3, 7:41 a.m. James (Sonny) Buchanan, 39, a landscaper, is shot and killed while mowing grass, only five miles from Martin's shooting

OCT. 3, 8:12 a.m. Premkumar Walekar, 54, a cabdriver, is killed while pumping gas, five miles northeast of the previous shooting and only 31 minutes later

OCT. 3, 8:37 a.m. Sarah Ramos, 34, a housekeeper, is killed while sitting on a park bench. A witness reports that a white van fled the scene, and a false trail begins

OCT. 3, 9:58 a.m. Lori Lewis Rivera, 25, a professional nanny, is killed while vacuuming her minivan outside a Shell station in Kensington, Md. It is the last of four lethal shootings to take place within a space of 2 hr. 20 min., all within the boundaries of Montgomery County, Md.

OCT. 3, 9:20 p.m. Pascal Charlot, 72, a retired handyman, is killed while crossing a street. The shooting takes place almost 12 hours after Rivera's murder and about a five-mile drive from the scene of that crime as much to speak to the snipers as to worried area residents.

As the manhunt intensified, the snipers settled into a grisly, if thankfully less frequent, staccato of killing. They returned to gas stations and targeted less populated areas, closer to major highways, which ensured quick getaways. The pair shot their ninth victim on the evening of Oct. 9, in Prince William Country, Va., east of the capital. They killed their 10th two days later, with a state trooper parked just across the way, in Fredericksburg, Va., 50 miles southwest of Washington. When witnesses again saw a white box truck or van near the scenes, authorities shut down local highways and concentrated on finding such a vehicle.

Even as they were concentrating on locating the phantom van, it later was discovered, police had stopped the snipers in their car in Washington on Oct. 3, the deadliest day of the rampage. But when they ran a standard check on the car, it came up clean, and the snipers moved on. Five days later, a Baltimore police officer again stopped the pair and checked the car; again nothing suspicious registered.

On Oct. 14, the killers struck again, fatally shooting FBI analyst Linda Franklin outside a Home Depot store in Falls Church, Va. Some witnesses saw a dark-colored sedan fleeing the area, but police homed in on one witness, who reported he had seen a cream-colored van. (The witness turned out to have fabricated the story; he was arrested.)

Yet even as the snipers were eluding the police dragnet, the strange psychological dance that often plays a part in serial killings was growing more intense. One or both of the snipers (this point was not initially made clear by police) began reaching out, almost as if seeking to be captured. On Oct. 17, a man identifying himself as the sniper called the police—one of thousands of such calls. The caller men-

SLAIN: The body of Linda Franklin lies in a Falls Church, Va., parking lot

GERALD HERBERT—THE WASHINGTON TIMES

OCT. 4, 2:30 p.m. Identity withheld: A 43-year-old mother of two is shot in the back while loading packages into her car in Fredericksburg, Va.—70 miles south of the previous incidents. She survives. It is the first shooting that does not occur in Maryland

OCT. 7, 8:08 a.m. Identity withheld: A 13-year-old boy is shot in the abdomen as he is dropped off at school. He survives. Police find a tarot "death" card at the scene

OCT. 9, 8:18 p.m. Dean Harold Meyers, 53, a Vietnam vet and architectural engineer, is killed while pumping gas at a Sunoco station in Manassas, Va., 35 miles from the capital

OCT. 11, 9:30 a.m. Ken Bridges, 53, a financier on a business trip, is killed in Fredericksburg, Va., about 50 miles southwest of Washington, also while pumping gas. A white van is again reported at the scene, putting more attention on a phantom vehicle

OCT. 12, 8:18 p.m. Chief Moose issues a composite image of a white truck sought in the crimes; police are also on the lookout for a white van

OCT. 14, 9:15 p.m. Linda Franklin, 47, an FBI intelligence analyst, is killed in the parking lot of a Home Depot store near Falls Church, Va. A press release from FBI Director Robert Mueller notes that some 400 agents were working on the investigation at the time of the murder

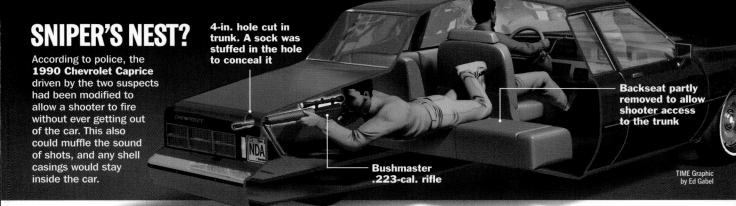

SNIPER'S NEST?

According to police, the **1990 Chevrolet Caprice** driven by the two suspects had been modified to allow a shooter to fire without ever getting out of the car. This also could muffle the sound of shots, and any shell casings would stay inside the car.

4-in. hole cut in trunk. A sock was stuffed in the hole to conceal it

Backseat partly removed to allow shooter access to the trunk

Bushmaster .223-cal. rifle

TIME Graphic
by Ed Gabel

---

tioned a crime in Montgomery, Ala., saying, "I did something down there." The next day, one of the snipers called the Rev. William Sullivan in Ashland, Va., raving, "I am God" and again referring to a crime in Alabama. Suspecting a prank, Sullivan did not report the call.

The snipers' contacts with the authorities now became more frequent: on Oct. 19, after shooting a 12th victim in Ashland, Va., the snipers left a letter demanding $10 million and rebuking the task force pursuing them for its "incompitence" [sic], noting that the call to Fr. Sullivan had not been pursued. The note ended with a chilling P.S.: "Your children are not safe anywhere at any time."

The next day, investigators interviewed Fr. Sullivan, who pointed them to Montgomery, Ala.. There, police recalled an unsolved September shooting of two women in a failed robbery of a liquor store; one of them died. When police ran a fingerprint from the scene through a national crime database, it matched the name of John Lee Malvo—and Malvo's file mentioned John Muhammad. For the first time, authorities had a solid lead. Still, on Oct. 22 the snipers struck again, killing a bus driver in Silver Spring, Md.—their 13th victim and 10th homicide. A second letter was found: it demanded that the $10 million be wired to a deactivated stolen credit card. Chief Moose went on TV to explain that this method of payment wasn't possible. The contretemps made area residents even more anxious; they knew the hunters and the hunted were straining, but failing, to reach a denouement.

But the police were now following up on significant evi-

SHANNON STAPLETON—POLARIS

ELATION: Chief Moose relaxes after the capture

dence. On Oct. 23, agents descended on the Tacoma, Wash., duplex where Malvo once lived, and retrieved a tree stump containing bullet fragments. That night, the police released the names of the suspects, along with a description of their car. Within a few hours—just before 1 a.m. on Oct. 24—trucker Ron Lantz spotted the Caprice, parked and silent, at an interstate rest stop outside Wheaton, Md. Two hours later, at 3:30 a.m., a massive police team rushed the car and awakened and arrested the two sleeping men. A Bushmaster .223 semiautomatic rifle was found in the car.

In retrospect, perhaps the most striking aspect of the case was just how off-target the pursuers' vision of their prey had been. As a top official told the New York *Times*: "Everyone thought we were looking for an angry white guy in a white van. Instead, it was really two black guys in a blue Chevy. We got stuck on that white van."

As prosecutors squared off over who would try the pair, police were linking them to a string of earlier violent crimes stretching from Washington State to the Southeastern U.S. Hundreds of questions surrounding the case remain unanswered. Did the men share in the shooting, or was one of them alone responsible? What, exactly, was their relationship—they often passed as kin, though they were not related. And which of the two had made the phone calls, spoken to Fr. Sullivan, written the notes? The answers would emerge, if slowly. For now, millions of residents of the D.C. area breathed more easily, knowing that the single most important question of them all—Are my streets safe?—had finally been resolved. ∎

OCT. 17
A sniper calls the police hot line and mentions a previous crime in Montgomery, Ala. On Oct. 18, a similar call is made to a priest. Neither the police nor the priest follow up

OCT. 19, 8:00 p.m.
Name Withheld, 37, a male, is shot as he leaves a restaurant in Ashland, Va. He survives. Police find a letter that berates them for not following up on the snipers' calls and demands $10 million

OCT. 21
Tipped off by the snipers' phone calls, police look into a failed robbery and murder in Alabama and identify both Malvo and Muhammad as suspects

OCT. 22, 6:00 a.m.
Conrad Johnson, 35, a bus driver, is killed while standing in his bus in Silver Spring, Md. He is the last of the snipers' 13 victims. A letter again demands $10 million

OCT. 23
Agents search Malvo's former home in Tacoma, Wash., above. That night, police release the names of both the suspects, along with a description of their car—a dark blue 1990 Chevrolet Caprice

OCT. 24, 3:30 a.m.
About 1 a.m., trucker Ron Lantz spots a car matching the description parked at an interstate rest stop and calls police. A massive team rushes the car, arrests the sleeping suspects without incident and finds a Bushmaster .223-cal. rifle, which matches ballistics tests from the snipers' bullets

ARIZONA: Ylie Blankenship, right, and Jack Fisher decide to hit the road

CALIFORNIA: The Copper fire shuts down a road north of Los Angeles

CALIFORNIA: Flames silhouette a fire fighter battling the McNally blaze

ARIZONA: The Rodeo-Chediski fire burns in an arc along a mountain

ARIZONA: Outside Forest Lakes, a plane drops chemical retardants

BURNING QUESTIONS

Who started the wildfires of 2002? And how many will burn in 2003?

YOU'RE NOT IMAGINING THINGS: HUGE, DEVASTATING wildfires—though an essential part of the life cycle of great forests—are burning through America's trees more frequently and with more power than before. The summer of 2000 was one of the worst ever recorded for the big blazes. Now, only two years later, frightening scenes of conflagration again dominated the news: homeowners fleeing just ahead of the flames, smokejumpers risking their lives to confine the damage, houses smoldering in ruins.

The fires of 2002 burned 6.6 million acres, compared with 8.4 million acres burned in 2000. But that's still about twice the 10-year average. After the punishing summer of 2000, Congress and the White House increased the number of the nation's army of fire fighters; some 18,000 of them were deployed in 2002, but they were still no match for the speed and intensity with which the infernos proliferated.

Acts of God? Certainly … except in Colorado, where, unthinkably, federal Forest Service agent Terry Barton admitted she deliberately started the flames that grew into the gigantic Hayman fire. The big blaze forced the evacuation of 8,000 people southwest of Denver and caused $38 million in damages. The largest burn in Colorado's history, it engulfed more than 136,000 acres, even as some 1,700 people battled the flames. Four Oregon fire fighters died when their van crashed while on the way to help fight it.

Barton confessed to authorities that on the afternoon of June 8, she got out of her truck, headed for a campfire circle, lighted a two-page letter from her ex-husband John that asked for a reconciliation, then left once it had burned. Soon after, she claimed, she returned to find grass burning, radioed for help and began containment efforts. On Dec. 6, Barton reached a plea bargain with federal prosecutors under which she agreed to plead guilty to two charges; she will probably spend six years in prison, rather than the 65 years she might have served under four original charges. She will be sentenced in February 2003. The federal charges to which she pleaded guilty each carries a fine of $250,000, but those fines and any restitution to victims of the fire were not included in the plea agreement. She is also very likely to face charges from the state of Colorado, prosecutors said.

But one case of alleged arson doesn't explain the summer's fires. Experts say several years of parched weather set the stage for the infernos. And since forecasters are predicting another dry winter, the odds are good that the summer of 2003 may find Americans once again all fired up. ∎

Profile

A Peacemaker's Reward

When former U.S. President Jimmy Carter was awarded the Nobel Prize for Peace in October, he celebrated in the no-frills manner that sets him apart from other ex-Presidents. Carter was in his tiny hometown of Plains, Ga., when he got the news, and a number of his friends and neighbors simply dropped by to give him congratulatory hugs. Carter has

HURLERS Coach Castro eyes Carter's hardball

dedicated his life after the presidency to a host of worthy causes: resolving international conflicts and promoting democratic elections around the globe; fighting disease in Africa; and promoting the charitable group Habitat for Humanity.

The Nobel Committee said it was honoring Carter's peacemaking activities both during and after his presidency, including the groundbreaking peace between Israel and Egypt he brokered at Camp David in 1978. Gunnar Berge, chair of the Nobel Peace Prize committee, initially claimed the honor was intended as a slap at President George Bush's bellicose policy toward Iraq, but other members quickly disavowed that view.

In May, Carter, who enjoys playing the role of gadfly, visited Cuba, where he shared a pitcher's mound with Fidel Castro—then pitched democracy and human rights to the Cuban people in an unprecedented hour of live, uncensored TV airtime.

SEARCHING Marsh, inset, hid bodies

A Macabre Find in Georgia

For years critics have been calling for better state and federal oversight of the funeral and crematory industries: only about half the states have some regulations governing these businesses. The concerns were vindicated in grisly fashion in February, when it was discovered that an undertaker in Noble, Ga., had not been cremating the dead consigned to him. Bodies were found stacked like firewood in piles of a dozen or more, jammed into sheds and buried

Roundup

FOUND: The body of Chandra Levy, the government intern, 24, who went missing in 2001, was found in Washington's Rock Creek Park in May. Evidence suggests she had been bound and then murdered

Crime and Punishment

Murder cases and murder trials made headlines in 2002, though one—the trial of Kennedy relative Michael Skakel—involved a crime that took place 27 years ago. In a more recent case, the body of government intern Chandra Levy, missing since the summer of 2001, was finally found. Police called her death a murder, but no arrests were made.

haphazardly in the backyard—340 bodies in all, in every state of decomposition.

Authorities arrested Ray Brent Marsh, 28, who had taken over the crematory from his father in 1996; he told police his incinerator had broken a while back—and that he just hadn't got around to fixing it. Marsh is charged with 16 counts of theft by deception, and could face 15 years in prison on each count.

A Rash of Kidnappings

America's parents—already jittery from terror attacks—found fresh reasons for concern in 2002, as a spate of child kidnappings sent shudders through the nation. Two girls from the same apartment complex in Oregon City, Ore., were abducted on their way to a bus stop,

MYSTERY: Four soldiers at the same military base, Fort Bragg in North Carolina, were accused of killing their wives in a seven-week period over the summer. Three of those accused were veterans of the Afghan conflict

GUILTY: In June, Michael Skakel, 41, Ethel Kennedy's nephew, was convicted of beating neighbor Martha Moxley, 15, to death in 1975

one in January, one in March. Danielle van Dam, 7, was kidnapped and murdered near San Diego in February. In June, Elizabeth Smart, 14, was abducted from her home in a Salt Lake City suburb. The same week a 14-year-old Idaho girl was abducted and chained to a bed. After she managed to escape, police staked out the kidnapper's house; he killed himself after a car chase.

SMART A poster appeal

The next month, Samantha Runnion, 5, was abducted, raped and murdered in gruesome fashion in Long Beach, Calif. Her alleged killer, Alejandro Avila, 27, had a history of molestation charges.

As of early December, Elizabeth Smart had not been located.

A Bomber's Pattern

A cross-country crime spree by a bomber who planted explosives in mailboxes injured six people and dredged up scary memories of both anthrax letters and the Unabomber. The unlikely culprit turned out to be 21-year-old Lucas Helder, a college student in Wisconsin. Helder seemed to seek arrest; he turned on the cell phone in his car on a Nevada highway, knowing it would be traced, after dispatching a

HELDER Just a spree?

18 bombs found in mailboxes since May 3

Suspect's home

Minn.

Nev.   Neb.   Iowa
         Colo.
                           Ill.

Suspect arrested May 7

Texas

600 miles
600 km

series of grandiose, threatening letters to his family.

It gets weirder: Helder told FBI agents his bombings were meant to draw an enormous smiley face across the map of the U.S. The first clusters of bombs in Illinois and Iowa and the second cluster in Nebraska, which had not been set to go off, made up the eyes; the mouth was to run from Colorado through Texas and beyond. Helder's friends were baffled; far from fitting the usual profile of an angry loner, he was considered easygoing. He will be tried in 2003 and could face 40 years—or even life—in prison.

All in the Family

R ichard Nixon came in for his share of gibes over the years, but his daughters Tricia, 56, and Julie, 53, have generally been admired for their graceful conduct during and after their father's troubles. The two were always close, but they made news in 2002 as adversaries in a dispute over the governance of the

Nixon Library in San Clemente, Cal.

Tricia's side wanted a small board dominated by the sisters, and the ouster of John Taylor, the library's long-serving director. Julie wanted to keep Taylor and a larger, independent board. The rift led to a lawsuit over the disposition of millions of dollars given to the library by wealthy Nixon pal Bebe Rebozo. When the mess hit the news, the sisters patched matters up and agreed to work together to garner funds for the institution, the only presidential library not granted an annual federal subsidy.

Image

Trail of Tears

A deadly passel of tornadoes swept across the nation from south to north on Nov. 10 and 11, killing 36 people in five states. Seventeen deaths were reported in Tennessee, 12 in Alabama, five in Ohio and one each in Mississippi and Pennsylvania. More than 200 people were injured.

The tiny eastern Tennessee town of Mossy Grove (pop. 200), left, was hit by a tornado packing 113-m.p.h. winds, which ripped a 200- to 300-yard-wide path right through the middle of the hamlet.

FEUDING? The Nixon sisters in 1995

SHERRON WATKINS•ENRON

COLEEN ROWLEY•FBI

Photograph for TIME by Gregory Heisler

CYNTHIA COOPER • WORLDCOM

Persons of the Year

Time Out! Three Gutsy Whistle-blowers Call Institutions to Account

They don't like to be called crusaders—and two out of three of them claim they hate the term whistle-blower. But each of them—Sherron Watkins of energy giant Enron, Coleen Rowley of the FBI and Cynthia Cooper of telecommunications leader WorldCom—took a stand in 2002, a year when some of America's most respected institutions proved to be not only fallible, but deceitful. For sounding the alarm on corruption and negligence in high places, and for asserting the primacy of truth in corporate and public life, they are TIME's Persons of the Year for 2002.

PERSONS OF THE YEAR

COLEEN ROWLEY | CYNTHIA COOPER | SHERRON WATKINS

2002 was the year when the grief started to lift and the
moods entered the room, two anxieties that rattled down
their particulars into the general disposition. To begin
of the pain, but every month or so there came a new

UNDER QUESTION **It was a year of institutional chiefs coming before Congress—FBI Director Robert Mueller; WorldCom's ex-CEO Be**

Bali, a surface-to-air missile fired at a passenger jet—that showed us the beast still at our door. In the confrontation with Iraq, in the contested effort to build a homeland defense, we all struggled to regain something like the more secure world we thought we lived in before the towers fell. But every step of the way we wondered, Was this the way back? What exactly did we need to be doing differently?

And all the while there was the black comedy of corporate fraud. Who knew that the swashbuckling economy of the '90s had produced so many buccaneers? You could laugh about the CEOs in handcuffs and the stock analysts who turned out to be fishier than storefront palm readers, but after a while the laughs came hard. Martha Stewart was dented and scuffed. Tyco was looted by its own executives. Enron and WorldCom turned out to be Twin Towers of false promises. They fell. Their stockholders and employees went down with them. So did a large measure of public faith in big corporations. Each new offense seemed to make the same point: with communism vanquished, capitalism was left with no real enemies but its own worst impulses. It can be undone by its own overreaching players. It can be bitten to pieces by its own alpha dogs.

Day after day, one set of misgivings twined around the other, depressing the stock market, giving the whole year its undeniable saw-toothed edge. Were we headed for a world where all the towers would fall? All the more reason to figure out quickly, before the next blow to the system, how to repair the fail-safe operations—in the boardrooms we trusted with our money, at the government agencies we trust with ourselves—that failed.

This is where three women of ordinary demeanor but exceptional guts and sense come into the picture. Sherron

Watkins is the Enron vice president who wrote a letter to chairman Kenneth Lay in the summer of 2001 warning him that the company's methods of accounting were improper. In January, when a congressional subcommittee investigating Enron's collapse released that letter, Watkins became a public figure, and the Year of the Whistle-Blower began. Coleen Rowley is the FBI staff attorney who caused a sensation in May with a memo to FBI Director Robert Mueller about how the bureau brushed off pleas from her Minneapolis, Minn., field office that Zacarias Moussaoui, who is now indicted as a Sept. 11 co-conspirator, was a man who must be investigated. One month later Cynthia Cooper exploded the bubble that was WorldCom when she informed its board that the telecommunications company had covered up $3.8 billion in losses through the prestidigitations of phony bookkeeping.

These women were for the 12 months just ending what New York City fire fighters were in 2001: heroes at the scene, anointed by circumstance. They were people who did right just by doing their jobs rightly—which means ferociously, with eyes open and with the bravery the rest of us always hope we have and may never know if we do. Their lives may not have been at stake, but Watkins, Rowley and Cooper put pretty much everything else on the line. Their jobs, their health, their privacy, their sanity—they risked all of them to bring us badly needed word of trouble inside crucial institutions. Democratic capitalism requires that people trust in the integrity of public and private institutions alike. As whistle-blowers, these three became fail-safe systems that did *not* fail. For believing—really believing—that the truth is one thing that must not be moved off the books, and for stepping in to make sure that

worries came in. During the first weeks of 2002, two dark everybody's nerve paths, even on good days, and etched with, after Sept. 11, the passage of time drew off the worst disturbance—an orange alert, a dance-club bombing in

and former CFO Scott Sullivan; Enron's ex-chairman Kenneth Lay; Lay takes the Fifth; Jeffrey Skilling, former CEO of Enron

it wasn't, they have been chosen by TIME as its Persons of the Year for 2002.

Who are these women?

For starters, they aren't people looking to hog the limelight. All initially tried to keep their criticisms in-house, to speak truth to power but not to Barbara Walters. They became public figures only because their memos were leaked. None of them had given an on-the-record media interview until TIME brought all three together in a Minneapolis hotel room in early December 2002. Very quickly it became clear that none of them are rebels in the usual sense. The truest of true believers is more like it, ever faithful to the idea that where they worked was a place that served the wider world in some important way. But sometimes it's the keepers of the flame who feel most compelled to set their imperfect temple to the torch. When headquarters didn't live up to its mission, they took it to heart.

What more do they have in common? All three grew up in small towns in the middle of the country, in families that at times lived paycheck to paycheck. In a twist that will delight psychologists, they are all firstborns. More unusually, all three are married but serve as the chief breadwinners in their families. Cooper and Rowley have husbands who are full-time, stay-at-home dads. For every one of the women, the decision to confront the higher-ups meant jeopardizing a paycheck their families truly depended on.

The joint interview in Minneapolis was the first time the three had met. But in no time they recognized how much they knew one another's experience. During the ordeals of this year, it energized them to know that there were two other women out there fighting the same kind of battles. In Minneapolis, when FBI lawyer Rowley heard Cooper talk about a need for regular people to step up and do the right thing, she stood up and applauded.

And what to make of the fact that all are women? There has been talk that their gender is not a coincidence; that women, as outsiders, have less at stake in their organizations and so might be more willing to expose weaknesses. They don't think so. As it happens, workplace studies show that women are a bit less likely than men to be whistle-blowers. And almost all whistle-blowers say they would not do it again. If they aren't fired, they're cornered: isolated and made irrelevant. Eventually many suffer from alcoholism or depression.

With these three, that hasn't happened, though Watkins left her job at Enron after a year when she wasn't given much to do. But ask them if they have been thanked sincerely by anyone at the top of their organization, and they burst out laughing. Some of their colleagues hate them, especially the ones who believe that their outfits would have quietly righted all wrongs if only they had been given time. "There is a price to be paid," says Cooper. "There have been times that I could not stop crying."

These were ordinary people who did not wait for higher authorities to do what needed to be done. Literature's great statement on unwelcome truth telling is Ibsen's play *An Enemy of the People.* Something said by one of his characters reminds us of what we admire about our Dynamic Trio. "A community is like a ship," he observes. "Everyone ought to be prepared to take the helm." When the time came, these women saw the ship in citizenship. And they stepped up to that wheel. ∎

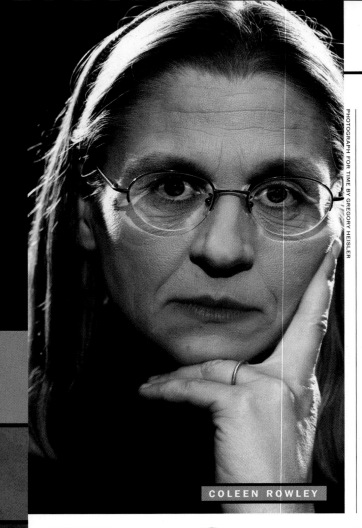

PHOTOGRAPH FOR TIME BY GREGORY HEISLER

COLEEN ROWLEY

to face cameras and Congressmen and that helped set off the debate over how to reinvent the FBI—was not meant to be a memo at all. It came tumbling out, almost by accident, because she couldn't hold the words inside anymore.

Since Sept. 11, the 48-year-old had muzzled her grief about the bureau's failures—specifically, about how it ignored cries from her office to take seriously the case of Zacarias Moussaoui, a French-Moroccan who spoke poor English and had signed up at a Minnesota flight school, keen to fly a 747. Eight months later, Rowley and others got a chance to speak. Staff members of the House and Senate Intelligence Committees' joint inquiry into the attacks invited her and others to come to Washington for a private interview.

After spending several frustrating days attempting to compose her testimony, Rowley had had enough. "I said, 'This is ridiculous. I'm on 36 hours without sleep. If I jot it down, first of all I won't forget it. And I won't have to keep reminding myself of things to say. I'll get it out of my system, and I'll be able to sleep.'" So she went to the office at 3 a.m. and sat at her desk writing until her husband Ross called 16 hours later, around 7 p.m.

By Monday morning, she had written 13 pages. This is more than just my own notes to myself, she decided. And she knew the memo was explosive enough for her to need some protection. Just $2\frac{1}{2}$ years from retirement and her family's sole breadwinner, she tacked on two sentences of self-preservation, asking for federal whistle-blower protection. At the time, she did not know exactly what it was—nor that the legislation offered FBI employees a weak shield.

The Special Agent

Coleen Rowley became enamored with the FBI's fictionalized ideal long before she heard of the real thing. Her favorite show was *The Man from U.N.C.L.E.*, a spy spoof about two debonair agents who work to save the world from evil. In the fifth grade, Rowley wrote to the show's producers, asking to join the cadre of supersecret spies. She got a letter saying the group didn't exist.

"But they told me that the U.S. had something called the FBI," Rowley recalls. "And they gave me the address."

So Rowley wrote to the bureau and got a pamphlet titled "99 Facts About the FBI." One question was, "Does the FBI employ women as special agents?" The answer was no. Even then, she did not scare easily. "I thought to myself, That's stupid. I figured that would change eventually."

In May, 2002, when Rowley upbraided her beloved FBI in a secret 13-page memo, she thought she was on a private rescue mission. In her view, it was not a reprimand but an act of redemption. The memo—the one that leaked and landed her in the newspapers, that brought her to Washington

The next day, in Washington, she dropped the memo off with receptionists for FBI Director Robert Mueller and two members of the Senate Committee on Intelligence. She had no appointments; she just wandered around until she found their offices, getting lost at least once. Then she walked outside and hailed a cab. "I went, 'Whew!' and collapsed in the back seat," Rowley remembers. Says her husband: "I remember her saying, 'I hope somebody reads it.'"

The next evening Rowley was back in the Minneapolis FBI office, working late. The designated representative had gone home, so Rowley got the call from CNN. A reporter had heard that someone from the office had written some kind of letter. Rowley, a 22-year veteran of the bureau, says she had never imagined that her name or her letter would get out, and was uncharacteristically speechless. "I said, 'Well, I can't help you. I don't know what you're talking about.' *Click!* And I ran out of the office."

And so it was that Rowley became the FBI's public conscience. Two weeks later, she was called back to Washington to testify in the open, her Coke-bottle glasses slipping down her nose, her circa-1985 hand-me-down plaid suit crying to be put back into the closet. She issued damning indictments—agents were drowning in paperwork and lived in fear of offending the higher-ups. "There's a certain pecking order, and it's pretty strong," she said. "It's very rare that someone picks up the phone and calls a rank or two above themselves." She offered specific solutions: Can you give us a computer system that allows us to search phrases like "flight schools"? And she was quick to admit what she did not know. When a senator asked her what advice she would give the President, she demurred. "I really can't presume to give advice at such a high level," she said. In short, she made the Congressmen look like interns on the set of the Coleen Rowley show. The only time she seemed perplexed during her D.C. visit was when a horde of reporters followed and shouted at her as she tried to hail a cab.

For Americans watching this odd display, the message was clear: This mid-level lawyer at a field office in the Midwest had higher expectations for the FBI than its top leaders. The bureau could be great, was her message, if only it put the goal of protecting Americans above the goal of protecting itself.

Seven months later, in December 2002, Rowley is still campaigning, albeit more warily. She talked to TIME, her first interview, with great trepidation. Afraid of being fired and afraid of appearing self-serving, she says: "I will not stand up in front of people unless I have something important to say." Visiting FBI headquarters after the hearing, she was popular with clerks and secretaries. In the Capitol building, janitors and police darted across the hall to thank her.

But the tough Rowley—the Rowley who packs a gun and takes it everywhere, who moves coatless through Minnesota winters and runs triathlons—has been stung by a nasty backlash within the FBI. In early June, an associate called to say high-level FBI agents in Washington had been overheard discussing possible criminal charges against her. Some fellow agents, retired ones in particular, crucified her. Charles George, then president of the Society of Former Special Agents of the FBI, compared her to convicted spy Robert Hanssen, calling her behavior "unthinkable" in the society newsletter. The backlash bit. Rowley knows the culture of loyalty is a defense mechanism, but she does not excuse it. "Loyalty to whomever you work for is extremely important. The only problem is, it's not *the* most important thing. And when it comes to not admitting mistakes, or covering up or not rectifying things only to save face, that's a problem."

So how did Rowley get so tough? In the tiny town of New Hampton, Iowa, where Rowley grew up, the socio-economic topography mirrors the geographical one: it's flat.

Everybody is on the level because there is only one. In the Iowa where she was raised and in the Apple Valley community outside Minneapolis where she moved with her family, hierarchy never had much of a chance.

So the girl who was informed at age 11 that she could not join the FBI went ahead and started the "World Organization of Secret Spies" with friends. She became known as someone who quietly righted small wrongs from the sidelines of the school, who bullied friends into doing something they didn't want to do.

After she put herself through college, Rowley went to law school at the University of Iowa, where she met her future husband Ross. And that's another tale of Rowley willfulness. He was balking at getting married, so Rowley told him she was joining the FBI and it was now or never. Two weeks later, they were wed, and soon after she was at the FBI Academy in Quantico, Va. Ross abandoned his studies in art history to follow her to Washington, and he has followed her around the world ever since, from New York City to Paris to Mississippi.

Rowley quickly made a mark. In 1984 she escorted the Colombo crime-family boss Gennaro Langella on his "perp walk" in front of the news cameras, and she helped keep tabs on other big-time mafiosi in New York City. In the '90s she won an FBI award for her work on the Andrew Cunanan case, a shooting rampage that started with two deaths in Minnesota and ended with the death of Gianni Versace in Miami.

Her hyperactivity at work is mirrored in her personal life. She walks fast with the long strides of a runner; she speaks without a filter—just a few words will set her off on a discourse about heart disease or what's wrong with the criminal-justice system. Her fiercest exclamations are

SEARING CRITIQUE Rowley's memo charges that FBI officials "glossed over" how much they knew about the possibility of an attack; below, the Twin Towers burn

SPENCER PLATT—GETTY IMAGES

PERSONS OF THE YEAR

COLEEN ROWLEY | **CYNTHIA COOPER** | **SHERRON WATKINS**

"Well, heck!" and "Oh, my gosh!" She often leaps to her feet to make a point, waves her arms, pounds her fist and attempts impersonations of the characters in her stories.

Rowley doesn't like to keep track of her keys, her purse or her four children. Ross has been a stay-at-home dad ever since Coleen was in training at Quantico and someone had to stay home with the baby. He pays the bills, fixes meals, sets the alarm clock and does the Christmas shopping. The night Rowley got the call from CNN, Ross had been watching a TV interview with a Senator. He could tell the man had read her memo from his comments. "I said, 'Oh, my gosh, he's read it!'" Ross recalls. As Coleen drove up the driveway, Ross ran down to meet her.

When Rowley walked into her office on the morning of Sept. 11 and saw the Twin Towers burning on TV, she immediately thought of Moussaoui. For three weeks her office had been trying—and failing—to get FBI headquarters to allow a request for a search warrant of his computer. Agents had had him arrested for overstaying his visa while

the country." Worrying that the new director had not been well briefed on the Moussaoui case, Rowley and her colleagues repeatedly tried to get a message to Mueller so he could modify his statements. But they received no response. After more information about the Moussaoui investigation became public, along with a memo from a Phoenix agent who had noted a pattern of Arab men signing up at flight schools, Mueller still insisted that the FBI could not have done anything to limit or prevent the destruction. Only after Rowley's memo was made public did Mueller revisit his assessment, with a feeble double negative: "I cannot say for sure that there wasn't a possibility we could have come across some lead that would have led us to the hijackers."

The experience may have cut into her faith, but it did not extinguish it. Rowley remains devoted to the FBI and is in many ways a dream employee. Because agents cannot accept gifts valued over $20, she paid TIME $30 to cover a dinner check. She has no tolerance for whining and, she

> **Washington**
>
> **Dear Director Mueller:**
>
> I feel at this point that I have to put my concerns in writing concerning the important topic of the FBI's response to evidence of terrorist activity in the United States prior to September 11th. The issues are fundamentally ones of INTEGRITY and go to the heart of the FBI's law enforcement mission and mandate. Moreover, at this critical juncture in fashioning future policy to promote the most effective handling of ongoing and future threats to United States citizens' security, it is of absolute importance that an unbiased, completely accurate picture emerge of the FBI's current investigative and m̲a̲n̲a̲gement strengths and failures.

they looked into his past. As Rowley wrote in her memo, French officials and other intelligence sources established that Moussaoui was affiliated with radical fundamentalist Islamic groups and activities connected to Osama bin Laden. Minneapolis agents pushed headquarters for approval to dig deeper, fearing—before Sept. 11—that he might be part of a larger scheme to hijack commercial jetliners. He has since been indicted as a co-conspirator.

We may never know whether the agents could have prevented the attacks if they had received the green light earlier, Rowley is quick to point out. "[But] it's at least possible we could have gotten lucky and uncovered one or two more of the terrorists in flight training prior to September 11th," Rowley wrote in her memo. And yet, three days after the attacks, Director Mueller expressed his shock that terrorists were training on U.S. soil: "The fact that there were a number of individuals that happened to have received training at flight schools here is news, quite obviously." Six days after the attacks, the rhetoric became even bolder. Said Mueller: "There were no warning signs that I'm aware of that would indicate this type of operation in

says, "I hate the term whistle-blower." She flatly rejects any suggestion that her warning memo has anything to do with her gender. "There are plenty of women who have been co-opted, who don't do the right thing. And there are plenty of men who do," she says. She half-jokingly asks everyone, from fellow agents to college students, if they'll come buy a burger from her one day if she gets fired. But she cannot seem to stop herself from going on to pitch those students on the job opportunities at the bureau. And she continues to send e-mails to headquarters suggesting investigative and legal strategies. None have received a substantive response. "I'm sure they think I'm crazy Coleen Rowley," she says.

Since her testimony, she has received hundreds of phone calls at her office from every kind of person who feels wronged by the criminal-justice system. Most have dubious claims. The few legitimate gripes do not generally fall under FBI jurisdiction. It is an enormous distraction, and it's clear she wishes the calls would stop. And yet Rowley feels obligated to check out every story. After all, she says, "they might have a point." ∎

CYNTHIA COOPER

In June 2002, Cooper told the audit committee of WorldCom's board that the company had been playing dirty with its accounting practices. She knew as she said it what would happen. Within days, the company fired its famed chief financial officer, Scott Sullivan, and told the world that it had inflated its profits by $3.8 billion—the largest accounting fraud in history. The number has since grown to $9 billion, and counting. Her colleagues have been handcuffed and led past TV cameras. Shareholders have lost some $3 billion, and by early 2003 at least 17,000 WorldCom employees will have lost their jobs.

Cooper, meanwhile, still drives to the desolate Clinton headquarters every day. She had spent her career trying to get the higher-ups to take her internal-auditing division seriously; it is only now, in bankruptcy, that WorldCom is finally doing so. Cooper, 38, a petite blond, has been given more money and twice as many staff members. Her division is probably the most secure at the company. And it is quite obvious that she is heartbroken.

Cooper went home to Clinton in 1991, leaving a career and a failed marriage in Atlanta. She had a 2-year-old daughter and needed a job fast. So she just picked up the phone and started calling CFOs. She got a job at World-Com—then named LDDS—as a contract employee making $12 an hour. After a brief stint at SkyTel, a paging company that would later be acquired by WorldCom, she returned to LDDS in 1994 to start the internal-audit depart-

The Night Detective

In Clinton, Miss., the

headquarters of WorldCom rises out of the moonscape of Waffle Houses and Pizza Huts like a dark steel mother ship. It is rather shocking to turn the corner and see it there, lurking behind the free-

way as if it had been teleported into this tiny town. In 1999 WorldCom founder Bernie Ebbers moved the company here, to his old college town, and everything changed. Employees started wearing their badges around town as a sign of their achievement. A Wal-Mart Supercenter sprang up. And millions of Ebbers' dollars went to making over Mississippi College. When friends came to visit Cynthia Cooper for lunch, she would give them a tour of the facility. This is the town where she had grown up, and she was proud of this company that knew no bounds. Cooper too had ridden the wave, becoming vice president of internal audit of what was, for a time, the 25th biggest company in the country.

ment. The company was precocious and growing fast, and though founder Ebbers and his team had little interest in the kind of financial nitpicking her division represented, Cooper says: "I loved it. It was a very exciting place to be. We were moving and shaking and acquiring companies."

Meanwhile, she reunited with the first man to have ever sent her a rose—Lance Cooper, the boy who had had an unrequited crush on her in high school. They were married in 1993. Lance had spent 12 years as a computer consultant but never found as much satisfaction in that job as he does today as a stay-at-home dad taking care of their kids Stephanie, 13, and Anna Katherine, 1.

When it was founded in 1983, LDDS was also a mom-and-pop operation. But in the 1990s, the little long-distance company matured into a powerhouse. In 1997 it shocked the industry with an unsolicited bid to take over MCI, a company more than three times its size. In 1998 *CFO Magazine* named Sullivan one of the country's best CFOs. At age 37 he was earning $19.3 million a year. The next year Cooper was promoted to vice president. The stock price was soaring, and she and her friends at work would sometimes talk of retiring early and living the good life.

But by early 2001, overexuberance for the telecom market had created a glut of companies like WorldCom, and earnings started to fall. Cooper was aware of the decline but not of the creative accounting fixes. At WorldCom her department handled operational audits, which set company budget standards and evaluated performance, among other things. Financial audits, which verify the accuracy of a company's financial reports, were the province of the then esteemed independent firm Arthur Andersen.

It was a fluke, really, that Cooper got wind of the rotten accounting. A worried executive in the wireless division told her in March 2002 that corporate accounting had taken $400 million out of his reserve account and used it to boost WorldCom's income. But when Cooper went to Andersen to inquire about the maneuver, she was told that it was not a problem. When she didn't relent, Sullivan angrily told Cooper that everything was fine and she should back off. Cooper, concerned that her job might be in jeopardy, cleared out personal items from her office.

But as the weeks went on, Cooper disobeyed Sullivan and directed her team members to widen their net. Hav-

Sullivan, known for his poker face, remained calm. He then asked her to delay the audit report, according to a World-Com timeline of events filed with the SEC. She told him that would not happen. The meeting was a turning point for her because she, like her colleagues in the industry, considered Sullivan to be an honest, gold-standard executive.

The next day, Cooper told the head of the audit committee about her findings, still hoping that there was a reasonable explanation. She and her team began looking for ways to somehow justify what they had found in the books. Finally, they confronted WorldCom's controller, David Myers, who admitted he knew the accounting could not be justified, according to an internal-audit memo. A showdown was set for June 20 in Washington, at an audit-committee meeting of WorldCom's board of directors.

At the meeting, Sullivan tried to explain the problems and asked for more time to fully support his argument. The committee members gave him the weekend. But he could not convince them. On June 24 the audit committee

SPEAK NO EVIL WorldCom's former top officers Bernie Ebbers, left, and Scott Sullivan, center, plead the Fifth at a congressional hearing

ing watched the Enron implosion and Andersen's role in it, she was worried they could not necessarily rely on the accounting firm's audits. So they decided to do part of Andersen's job over. She and her team began working late into the night, keeping their project secret. And they had no allies. At one point, one of Cooper's employees bought a CD burner and started copying data, concerned that the information might be destroyed before they could finish.

Late in May, Cooper and her group discovered a gaping hole in the books. In public reports the company had categorized billions of dollars as capital expenditures in 2001, meaning the costs could be stretched out over a number of years into the future. But in fact the expenditures were for regular fees WorldCom paid to local telephone companies to complete calls and therefore were not capital outlays but operating costs, which should be expensed in full each year. It was as if an ordinary person had paid his phone bills but written down the payments as if he were building a phone tower in his backyard. The trick allowed WorldCom to turn a $662 million loss into a $2.4 billion profit in 2001.

On June 11, Sullivan called Cooper and gave her 10 minutes to come to his office and describe what her team was up to, says a source involved with the case. She did, and

told Sullivan and controller Myers that they would be terminated if they did not resign before the board meeting the next day. Sullivan refused to step down and was fired. Myers resigned. The next day, WorldCom came clean about its books. In August, Sullivan was indicted on charges of securities fraud. He could face up to 65 years in prison.

Meanwhile, Cooper was losing control over her domain at WorldCom. One day she walked into the office and found eight investigators perusing her files. All her phone and e-mail messages are being collected, to this day. Yet Cooper says she is encouraged by the changes at her firm. The company has carried out many of her recommendations. She has received more than 100 letters and e-mails from strangers who want to thank and encourage her. But she has not been personally thanked by a single senior executive at WorldCom, her colleagues say.

In November, WorldCom's new CEO, Michael Capellas, held a rally to try to light a spark in the demoralized World-Com work force. He called members of his management team onto the stage, and the all-male ensemble sang, "If you're happy and you know it, clap your hands!" Cooper was not there; the rally was in Virginia, and she was back in Mississippi, with her team, watching via webcast. ■

PHOTOGRAPH FOR TIME BY GREGORY HEISLER

SHERRON WATKINS

The Party Crasher

On Feb. 13, 2002, the

day before she presented the first of two damning testimonials to Congress, Enron vice president Sherron Watkins spent the afternoon in a cluttered conference room in the Rayburn House building on Capitol Hill. It was a cram session, a last

chance for Watkins, her attorney and congressional staff members to review the dozens of subpoenaed documents she would be quizzed on the next day. As they ate cold pizza, someone drew her attention to an e-mail titled "Confidential Employee Matter" that had been written by one of Enron's external lawyers. "Per your request," it began, "the following are some bullet thoughts on how to manage the case with the employee who made the sensitive report." Her eyes skipped down the page: "Texas law does not currently protect corporate whistle-blowers. The Supreme Court has twice declined to create a cause of action for whistle-blowers who are discharged ..."

Her pulse quickened. "I'm reading this and I'm thinking, Oh, my God, it's [dated] two days after I met with Ken Lay. Talk about shoot the messenger. I can't believe they looked into firing me," she says, sounding wounded even now in the retelling. "It was a horrible response. There's nothing in there to remind them to remember the code of conduct, the vision and values." This was how hard Watkins had fallen for Enron. Here she was, almost six months to the day since she first warned chairman Kenneth Lay of "an elaborate accounting hoax." Her boss had long ago confiscated her hard drive, and she had been demoted 33 floors from her mahogany executive suite to a "skanky office" with a rickety metal desk and a pile of make-work projects. But still, Watkins could not fathom that this company, the one she had tried to save from itself, had considered taking away the job she loved.

The next morning Watkins appeared before the tangle of cameras and for five hours patiently explained the intricacies of the financial schemes that had allowed the energy giant to conceal billions of dollars of debt in dubious partnerships. She was relaxed, even witty. But her square jaw clenched whenever she spoke about her company. She firmly indicted several top executives, yet she insisted that Lay was a "man of integrity." And she spoke almost wistfully of Enron's people, "energized to change the world." It was Valentine's Day, and she was still very much in love.

For months afterward, Watkins faithfully went to work each day, looking on as Enron auctioned off everything down to the sign at its headquarters (price: $44,000) and as the firm's esteemed accountants, Arthur Andersen, went down in their own wave of scandal. In November 2002, she left her $165,000 job. But her future is shaky. She plans to start a consulting firm to advise company boards on governance and ethics. She has been earning up to $25,000 on the speaking circuit and shared a $500,000 advance to co-author a book.

Watkins' independent streak came from her mother, who graduated from the University of Texas at Austin magna cum laude with dual degrees in education and accounting, then taught high school business. When Watkins was 14, her parents divorced and money grew tight. Her mother stopped buying ice cream and began limiting the kids to one pair of shoes each. At 16, Watkins started working the register at her uncle's market and helped put herself through the University of Texas at Austin, where she earned a degree in accounting. She took a job at Arthur Andersen and, after a stint in the Houston office, put in for a transfer to New York City. "New York kind of toughens you up for people doing the right thing," she says. "It almost makes you call bulls___ faster."

Such impudence, while a virtue in New York, was less appreciated when she returned to Houston in 1993 to take a job with Enron. Her mother noted the new attitude. And while Watkins rose quickly through the ranks, she earned a well-deserved reputation for lack of tact. Poised and pleasant with clients, Watkins often barreled right through her colleagues. They nicknamed her the "Buzz Saw."

By the time Watkins arrived, Enron was fast shedding its image as a staid natural-gas-pipeline company. Trading chief Jeffrey Skilling and his financial whiz, Andrew Fastow, wanted to build a nimble, "asset-light" firm that could exploit deregulating markets for energy, water, weather derivatives, broadband capacity and anything else that could be turned into a commodity. The strategy spawned explosive growth. By 2000, Enron was the seventh largest company in America. The '90s were fat times for Enron, and the corporate culture oozed in excess. The company rented ski condos in Beaver Creek, Colo., and stocked each with a personal chef. Christmas parties were multimillion-dollar, black-tie affairs with ice sculptures.

"The reason people love Enron is because there was re-

when Lay held a company-wide meeting and didn't allude to her concerns, she arranged a face-to-face appointment for Aug. 22 and drafted a longer, seven-page memo to hand to Lay. It was even more cataclysmic than the first.

Meanwhile, Watkins was getting jumpier. She was waking up at 2 a.m. rehearsing what she would say to Lay. Yet the meeting proved relatively uneventful. Lay seemed composed but genuinely concerned and said he would have attorneys look into the questionable deals. Watkins left feeling buoyed. For the first time that week, she slept through the night. In late September, even after netting $1.5 million by exercising personal stock options, Lay told Enron employees that "our financial liquidity has never been stronger." Not so. By mid-October, the company announced a $618 million third-quarter loss and a $1.2 billion write-off, tied to the murky partnerships that had worried Watkins. On Dec. 2, Enron filed for Chapter 11.

When her name was leaked in early January, Watkins initially felt a rush. She signed autographs in Starbucks; her

IN THE SPOTLIGHT **Watkins testified before the Senate with Enron's former CEO Jeffrey Skilling and then president Jeffrey McMahon**

ally no defining organizational structure," says Watkins. "If you wanted to start something and go for it, you could." One month she was in Panama sizing up a copper mine, the next she was in Hong Kong financing a nickel deal. Enron was a pressure cooker that "ranked and yanked" employees every six months, yet Watkins thrived on the pace.

But by spring 2001, the technology bubble was bursting, and Enron was slipping along with it. In late June, Watkins went to work directly for Fastow, who charged her with finding assets to sell off. Yet everywhere she looked she found fuzzy off-the-books deals that seemed to be backed by nothing more than now deflated Enron stock. No one she asked could—or cared to—explain what was really going on. Knowing that others had got into trouble after challenging Skilling, now CEO of the entire company, Watkins began scouting for a new job, hoping to confront Skilling on her last day at Enron.

But on Aug. 14, Skilling abruptly quit, and Lay invited employees to put any concerns in a comment box. The next morning Watkins sat at her computer and tapped out her first anonymous one-page memo in a single two-hour flourish. "I am incredibly nervous that we will implode in a wave of accounting scandals," she wrote. But the next day,

husband Rick, a vice president with Canadian Superior Energy, jokingly referred to himself as "Mr. Sherron Watkins." One morning a maintenance crew arrived to move her back up to an executive office. But the high was short-lived. Some laid-off Enron employees fumed that soon after writing her memos, Watkins unloaded $47,000 in Enron stock—moves she says were motivated by advice from her accountant and post-9/11 jitters. By far the most intense criticism has centered on Watkins' decision to sell her story in book and movie deals and on the lecture circuit.

But in her speeches, Watkins calls for reforms in the structure of corporate governance. She hopes her book will "cleanse the résumés of the good people at Enron." And she has to make a living. She has always paid most of the bills, and in September, Rick quit his job to spend more time with the family. Now she brings home the only paycheck.

Still, Watkins has no regrets. Late in 2002, she found a green Enron note pad that features a quote from Martin Luther King Jr.: "Our lives begin to end the day we become silent about things that matter." She smacked her palm against her forehead. "You look at it and you think, 'Oh, my God, look how many people at Enron stayed silent,'" she says. "That's what they wrote. And nobody listened." ∎

The Interview

On a Saturday morning in December 2002, TIME invited Cynthia Cooper of WorldCom, Coleen Rowley of the FBI and Sherron Watkins of Enron to talk about their experiences over the past year. The women had never met before.

TIME: How do you explain why so many people at your organizations did not do what you did?

WATKINS: I think it's the value system at the top. It's very important that the leaders set the tone. Remember the Tylenol-tampering scare? It threw the company into a tailspin. [But] the chairman came in, supposedly, and said, "We have got to do the right thing. We are pulling every bottle of Tylenol off the shelves worldwide." It cost them $300 million to do, but they set the standard for tamper-resistant products, and in the long run he saved consumer loyalty.

TIME: Why didn't those at the upper echelons admit their mistakes?

WATKINS: It's ingrained in human nature to fight and argue. My 3-year-old won't say she's sorry. She'll sit in time-out forever.

ROWLEY: It's worse in the U.S., with the adversary system and hiring lawyers. No one does anything wrong anymore.

TIME: If the culture comes from the top, why didn't you three fall prey to it?

COOPER: I think it comes back to values and ethics that you learn through your life. I think this is a wake-up call for the country. There's a responsibility for all Americans—teachers, mothers, fathers, professors, corporate people—to make sure the moral and ethical fabric of the country is strong.

ROWLEY: [Stands up and bursts into applause] I don't care if you're an FBI agent or a priest or a government official. We are all human, and we are all susceptible to any number of vices and mistakes. All we can do is try to uncover and correct them.

TIME: Are you known as people who admit when they're wrong?

ROWLEY: [After a pause] I'm trying to think if I have ever been wrong. [Laughter all around.] I don't think I am exceptional. I think everyone makes mistakes.

TIME: Would any of you go back and change anything you did?

WATKINS: I wouldn't not do it. [But] what I really failed to grasp was the seriousness of the emperor-has-no-clothes phenomenon. I thought leaders were made in moments of crisis, and I naively thought that I would be handing [Enron chairman] Ken Lay his leadership moment. I honestly thought people would step up. But I said he was naked, and when he turned to the ministers around him, they said he was clothed.

TIME: All of you shy away from discussing the fact that you're all women, but other people notice it at once. Why do you three think there's no connection?

WATKINS: I do think there's something to being a woman. There's a little bit of a boys' club, whether it's the golf or the sports talk. I am really uncomfortable with making general statements. But men are more reluctant to put their friends in jeopardy. I don't necessarily want friendships in the workplace. I think most men have no friendships outside the workplace. [Also] society doesn't ask women what you do for a living. Your ego or self-worth isn't [as] tied to what you do.

TIME: Did you love your jobs?

ROWLEY: The idea of a law-enforcement group that is able to solve a crime, get the bad guy and ideally even prevent the crime from occurring? Honestly, I would not want to do anything else. All agents join the FBI with that in mind. We are the good guys. The sad thing is, at some point you see the warping of it, the overlegalization of it, the gaming of the criminal-justice system.

WATKINS: It's disheartening to see that the FBI has as many problems as corporate America. In this country, we have a vacuum in leadership. We value the wrong people. Warren Buffett is boring, but he didn't invest in tech stocks because he didn't understand how they made money. He was right. But we value splashy leaders.

COOPER: People who move to the top are typically racehorses, not workhorses. And they're very charismatic.

WATKINS: And the dark side of charisma is narcissism.

TIME: What was the reaction to you in the workplace and on the street?

WATKINS: Early on, there were hundreds of e-mails, voice-mails, letters from the Enron rank-and-file employees. There was a sense of overwhelming relief because they had thought the top executives would get away with it. People were were pumped. Now no one recognizes me.

ROWLEY: In Minnesota, people get over these things really fast. It's over. This fame thing is greatly overrated.

TIME: Have any of you been thanked?
[All three women dissolve into uncontrollable laughter.] ■

Photograph by Frederic Lafargue—Gamma

Dreams of Peace Seem Far Away As Bloodshed Rules the Middle East

It was March 11, 2002—the six-month anniversary of the deadly terrorist attacks on America. Even as U.S. allies gathered at the White House to celebrate their success in fighting the war on terror, the long-running conflict in the Middle East erupted in new fury. Responding to suicide bombings of civilians, 40 Israeli tanks and 100 armored personnel carriers rumbled into the West Bank town of Ramallah, Yasser Arafat's headquarters. As Israeli troops machine-gunned Arab homes, an Arab mob killed a suspected collaborator, then hanged his body by the feet. Here, Palestinians hold their position, seemingly exhorted by a poster of Yasser Arafat.

WAR OF NERVES

George Bush pressures Iraq's Saddam Hussein: will a conflict follow?

SIC SEMPER TYRANNIS: THAT WAS THE EPITAPH AMERICA and its allies prepared to carve on Saddam Hussein's headstone as Iraqi forces reeled backward through the desert in retreat from Kuwait in the early weeks of 1991. But President George Bush and his foreign policy advisers surprised just about everyone by bringing the Gulf War to an unexpectedly swift conclusion. The campaign ended with half the victory the world had been led to expect—Kuwait liberated but the tyrant of Baghdad still in place—and a sense of unfinished business clouded the valedictories. Now, a dozen years later, the son of the President who stopped short of marching into Baghdad sat in the Oval Office and contemplated the prospect—and the price—of finishing the campaign that his father began.

In February 1991, it would have been difficult to predict that Saddam Hussein could survive to cause trouble in 2002. Yes, the Kuwaiti oil fields he had coveted, conquered and lost were set ablaze by retreating Iraqi troops at his command, but this seemed like the last, desperate act of a despot whose time had run out.

Both Saddam's northern and southern flanks were in trouble. To the north, just inside Iraq's border with Turkey, waited the Kurds, the world's largest ethnic group without their own homeland, who longed to carve a new country out of Iraq's territory. To the south, the Shi'ites massed on the Iranian border. Armed and encouraged by their co-religionists in Tehran, they were eager to topple Saddam's secular Suuni regime and spread Islamic revolution to Iraq and throughout the Middle East. Both groups were cheered on by President Bush, who urged Saddam's domestic enemies to rise up against him, implying that U.S. support would be forthcoming. It was not. When both Kurd and Shi'ite groups began insurrections, they were massacred by the thousands, and coalition troops did not intervene.

But this somber note was drowned out by the fanfare surrounding the coalition victory. Saddam seemed perma-

IT'S PERSONAL: In 2002 George Bush said of Iraq's leader: "I hate Saddam Hussein. I don't hate a lot of people. I don't hate easily, but his word is no good, and I think he's a brute"

sassinate former President Bush was uncovered. In 1994 Iraq again massed troops on Kuwait's border; they dispersed only after the U.S. dispatched 54,000 troops and an aircraft carrier battle group to the region. U.S. cruise missiles struck Iraqi missile facilities in 1996 after an Iraqi incursion into the Kurds' "safe haven" in the north.

In 1997 U.N. arms monitors reported that Iraq was still hindering inspections and sheltering banned weapons programs. Finally, in 1998, Saddam declared that U.N. arms monitors were no longer welcome in Iraq. The Security Council condemned Iraq's "flagrant violation" of U.N. resolutions, while the U.S. and Britain announced preparations for an attack. But apart from four days of air strikes, nothing was done. For two years, with the occasional exception of shooting in the no-fly zone, the U.S. and U.N. left Saddam to his own devices.

THEN, IN A SINGLE DAY, THE WORLD CHANGED. AFTER Sept. 11, 2001, Saddam's long history of involvement with terrorist organizations suddenly looked much more sinister. Following the anthrax attacks after 9/11, the fact that Iraq is known to have accumulated vast stockpiles of the disease agent both frightened and outraged the American public. And U.S. intelligence officials were intrigued by reports that lead hijacker Mohammed Atta had met with an Iraqi intelligence operative in Prague shortly before 9/11—though the reports were never verified. In short, to the White House, Iraq suddenly looked like a problem that could no longer be ignored.

George W. Bush devoted much of the year 2002 to painting Saddam Hussein's Iraq as an outlaw nation that was developing and storing huge quantities of weapons of mass destruction. Bush urged America's allies and the U.N. to demand a robust new round of inspections to assess Iraq's arsenal—and made it clear that if Saddam did not agree, the U.S. was prepared to go to war to disarm him or even foment "regime change" in Iraq. Moreover, Bush declared, he was prepared to wage that war alone, if necessary. By year's end, Bush got his way. U.N. inspectors were in Iraq, probing for weapons caches. Their presence was the result of two battles: an internal struggle between hawks and doves within the President's foreign policy team, and a diplomatic effort to win the support of the U.N. and America's allies for the inspections.

nently handcuffed by the terms of a cease-fire that stripped his armed forces of all but conventional weapons, mandated a stiff regimen of weapons inspections, kept crippling economic sanctions in place and imposed a no-fly zone in the north to prevent Saddam's air force from annihilating the Kurds. A similar protective umbrella was slapped over Shi'ite havens in southern Iraq in the summer of 1992.

In some ways, though, the war with Iraq never really ended: since 1991, a stutter-step of confrontations has hectored the peace. Coalition warplanes and ships attacked both missile sites and an Iraqi nuclear facility late in 1992. Six months later, U.S. naval vessels fired 24 cruise missiles at Baghdad's intelligence headquarters after an abortive plot to as-

INSULT: Visitors to Baghdad get a chance to walk on a portrait of Bush

The President began his campaign against Saddam in his January State of the Union address, in which he declared that "Iraq continues to flaunt its hostility toward America and to support terror." He grouped Iraq with Iran and North Korea as members of an "axis of evil."

But almost as important as what Bush said was what he left unsaid. Skeptics asked which changed circumstances or new information made Iraq suddenly more dangerous, or war with Saddam suddenly more necessary? As no one on Bush's team seemed prepared to explain what exactly Iraq had to do with Osama

NUCLEAR SITE? Iraq's al-Qaim phosphate plant, photographed in September 2002, is suspected of being a uranium-extraction facility. Iraqis admitted in December they had sought to build a nuclear weapon in the past but claimed they had abandoned the effort in recent years

bin Laden, critics pointed out that tracking down the mastermind of the 9/11 attacks might take years, while Iraq seemed a comparatively easy target at which to vent American anger. Yet at the same time, the Iraqi leader's well-documented misdeeds helped defuse criticism of Bush. It was difficult for anyone to deny that the world would be better off with Saddam out of power—or, at the least, declawed. Thus the argument came to center not so much on the end—inspecting, disarming or even removing Saddam—as on the means of doing the job.

A phalanx of Administration hawks—Vice President Dick Cheney, Defense Secretary Donald Rumsfeld and Deputy Defense Secretary Paul Wolfowitz—argued for quick military action. Quietly leading those who favored a more considered approach was Secretary of State Colin Powell, who believed that continued economic sanctions and renewed weapons inspections could accomplish as much as war, at a much lower price. He also argued that the U.S. should proceed in tandem with the U.N. and its allies, rather than acting unilaterally. It is perhaps telling that each of the hawks was a veteran of the first Bush

Administration, and had argued during the Gulf War for more precipitate action, whereas Powell (then head of the Joint Chiefs of Staff and the only professional soldier in the group) had argued for a later start date and an early end to hostilities. Oddly for an Administration that is usually tight-lipped, some of the internal White House debate was conducted in public, when Pentagon war plans were leaked. And in an August piece in the *Wall Street Journal*, Brent Scowcroft, the respected National Security Adviser to the elder George Bush, opposed the President's strategy.

In Europe and the Middle East, Bush faced a situation that was anything but encouraging. In the midst of a hotly contested election, German Chancellor Gerhard Schröder strongly distanced his nation from the possibility of a new Gulf War. In August, French President Jacques Chirac spoke out against Bush's policy. Longtime Arab allies also urged Bush to stop talking about war: Saudi Arabia made it clear that U.S. bases in the kingdom could not be used to launch an attack against neighboring Iraq.

But the President was not to be deterred. He continued pressing his case both at home and abroad, stressing the dangers of an Iraq armed with weapons of mass destruction. By the fall, he was finding traction—and the debate within his Administration had been resolved. Powell prevailed in his argument to conduct the campaign against Iraq via diplomacy, not war, at least for now. One day after the first anniversary of the 9/11 attacks, the President challenged the U.N. General Assembly, saying, "Will the United Nations serve the purpose of its founding—or will it be irrelevant?" Four days later, Baghdad agreed to allow inspections to resume at an unspecified time. It seemed a ploy designed to buy time and divide Saddam's enemies.

On Oct. 11, both houses of Congress passed a resolution authorizing the President to use military force in Iraq, with or without U.N. approval. Democrats read the mood of their constituents and overwhelmingly voted with the President. On Nov. 8, the U.N. Security Council unanimously approved a U.S.-drafted compromise resolution that required Iraq to submit to new weapons inspections and warned of "serious consequences" for noncompliance. It was a huge victory for Bush. France, Germany, Russia—and even Syria—were now onboard. Within days, Iraq formally agreed to the new U.N. inspection terms.

At home, Bush had now won congressional approval to launch a strike against Saddam without a declaration of war. Abroad, he had won both a new round of tough inspections and protection from the charge that the U.S. would be acting alone, heedless of world opinion.

Momentum among America's allies continued to turn in Bush's favor in the fall. Once re-elected, Schröder said that Germany would serve as a staging area in any war against Iraq; France ceased its public criticism of Bush. The tide crested at the NATO summit late in November, which ended with a unanimous declaration supporting the U.N. stance. The allies seemed to have decided that joining Bush's team would give them some leverage over him. And he won points by saying, "Contrary to my image as a Texan with two guns on my side, I'm more comfortable with a posse."

O N NOV. 25, A TEAM OF 23 U.N. INSPECTORS ARRIVED in Baghdad; two days later, they began their work. Within days, they had visited 22 suspected weapons sites. To no one's surprise, they found nothing suspicious at first. There are some 1,000 sites to be searched, and some 100 more inspectors were due to arrive by year's end, as well as helicopters to extend the range of the probe. Such visits, however, rarely produce dramatic moments of discovery. In the past, arms were tracked down mostly by piecing together complex mosaics from satellite pictures and surveillance cameras or via intelligence from defectors. As U.S. experts pointed out, Iraq could be hiding chemical devices in wells or residential basements. Or shuffling around tiny quantities of biotoxins in movable, undetectable vans, as if playing three-card monte.

On Dec. 7, per the U.N. resolution, Iraq submitted an inventory of its arsenal, as well as chemical, biological and nuclear programs it claimed were peaceful—and said it had no weapons of mass destruction. The declaration was on a computer disk; printed out, it ran to 12,000 pages. Said Richard Butler, head of the 1998 inspection team: "Dump-

THE PUSH TO INSPECT

ALLIES: Bush meets U.N. Secretary-General Kofi Annan, who advised against unilateral U.S. action, on Nov. 13, the day the Iraqis formally agreed to U.N. inspections

■ **March:** Iraq and a U.N. team confer to put in place a new round of weapons inspections. The talks fail, as do further meetings in May, July and August.

■ **May:** The U.N. Security Council votes unanimously to revamp its sanctions against Iraq, speeding delivery of food and medicine and tightening the military embargo.

■ **September:** Speaking to the U.N. General Assembly, George Bush urges a tough, united line on Iraq but warns that the U.S. is willing to act alone if necessary.

■ **October:** Bipartisan majorities in both houses of Congress authorize Bush to use military force, if needed, to disarm Iraq. Saddam Hussein is "re-elected" Iraq's President. The tally: 11 million to 0.

■ **November:** The U.N. Security Council unanimously approves a U.S.-drafted resolution to disarm Iraq that does not explicitly authorize the use of force. Iraq agrees to inspections, two days before the U.N. deadline. On Nov. 25, U.N. weapons inspectors arrive in Baghdad to begin their work and meet no opposition.

■ **December:** Iraq releases a 12,000-page list of its current weapons and those in development

NO WAR! Bush's threats against Saddam galvanized the strongest U.S. peace movement since Vietnam days

ing a truckload of material is part of the process of obfuscation." Iraq complained that under the wording of the U.N. resolution, a single inaccurate fact in this document could constitute a "material breach" of the resolution—and that such a breach could be used as a justification for war against Iraq. No one in the Bush Administration bothered to dispute that claim. In fact, the inspections were barely under way when Bush pronounced them "not encouraging." The President said disarmament, not inspections, was the goal, and the burden was on Saddam to prove Iraq was defanged.

One purpose of the heated rhetoric was to convince Saddam that he was on the brink of war, so he would have every incentive to comply with inspectors' requests. The U.S. hoped the tough tone would pre-empt any positive reaction to Iraq's appearance of cooperation, which might erode international readiness to take up arms against him.

The harsh words also reflected the deep resistance lingering in some parts of the Administration to letting inspections proceed at all. The hard-liners never supported the U.N. mission and regarded inspections as an impediment to war. The moderates argued that an inspections effort working its way methodically to the irrefutable conclusion that Saddam has not disarmed was the only way the U.S. could muster allies for war.

But on one point, both sides could agree: one way or another, Saddam would be disarmed. To drive the point home— even as U.N. personnel began to pry and poke at Iraq's arsenal—the U.S. military was ramping up its presence in the gulf. General Tommy Franks, head of the U.S. Central Command, and more than 600 officers from his Florida headquarters set up a forward command post in Qatar, joining U.S. personnel already on the ground in Bahrain, Kuwait, Yemen, Oman and the United Arab Emirates.

In all, more than 30,000 Americans in uniform were within striking distance of Iraq by Dec. 1, with an additional 45,000 ready to join them on short notice. Two carrier battle groups were also in the region; three more were due to join them by Dec. 15. As the TIME Annual closed this story on Dec. 12, the prospect of another President Bush sending American troops into battle against Saddam Hussein seemed very real. ■

WEAPONS IN A HAY

Finding Iraq's illegal arms will be immensely difficul U.N. inspectors will have to probe 750 known sites fo chemical, biological and nuclear weapons and missile and uncover uncounted new ones

THE TASK OF THE INSPECTORS ...

Under the terms of existing Security Council resolutions, two organizations field teams o experts in everything from biological agents to satellite imagery and nuclear weapons systems. But there are fewer than 200 inspectors to scrutinize an area the size of Califor

U.N. Monitoring, Verification and Inspection Commission (UNMOVIC)

Hans Blix

Headed by legal expert and former atomic-agency director Hans Blix, UNMOVIC was authorized under softer terms after the former U.N. inspection team, UNSCOM, was barred from Iraq in December 1998. Since then, Blix has assembled 220 experts from 45 countries: 80 at a time will work from Baghdad using five helicopters. Personnel include military specialists, biochemists and engineers, all seconded to U.N. employ and financed by a tax on Iraq's U.N.-run oil-for-food program

CHEMICAL
Although an extensive arsenal, including 690 tons of a chemical weapons agent, was destroyed by UNSCOM, Iraq may still have a stockpile of chemical-weapons munitions and the ingredients to produce weaponized mustard gas, VX and other nerve agents

BIOLOGICAL
The biggest, scariest unknown in Saddam's arsenal: inspectors know 17 tons of biological-weapons growth culture for making anthrax was unaccounted for in previous inspections, and suspect much more like it is out there

MISSILE
More than 800 Scuds were destroyed, but Iraq is believed to have secreted one or two dozen on mobile launchers somewhere in the desert. Iraq may be importing parts to expand its legal 150-km missiles to 600-km range

International Atomic Energy Agency (IAEA)

Jacques Baute

Jacques Baute, a French nuclear-weapons scientist, heads the separate team that searches out nukes. He can field more than 15 IAEA professionals from 11 countries, with possible help from 15 outside experts, who monitor all stages of the nuclear fuel cycle by looking for 40 specific components and analyzing soil and water samples, as well as checking on dual-use technologies, import-export controls and nuclear smuggling

NUCLEAR
By 1998, Iraq's nuclear program had been successfully dismantled. Since then, it has rebuilt facilities and equipment, worked on producing enriched uranium and shopped the black market to try to buy it

SYRIA

JORDAN

SMUGGLING

... AND A FEW PLACES THEY WILL HAVE TO LOOK

PRESIDENTIAL COMPOUNDS
More commonly known as palaces, these huge complexes are believed to hide important research labs. In the past, access to the compounds was severely restricted

MOBILE LABS AND MISSILES
Much of Iraq's secret weapons work is now mobile, allowing it to be moved before inspectors see it. Some illegal longer-range missiles are hidden on mobile launchers

ACK

TURKEY

Al 'Amadiyah

Dahuk

Rawanduz

Tall 'Afar

Mosul

Arbil   Kuysanjaq

IRAN

NORTHERN NO-FLY ZONE

Tigris River

Kirkuk

As-Sulaymaniyah

Ba'iji

Tikrit

Khanaqin

Euphrates River

Anah

Lake Ath-Tharthar

Al Hadithah

Al-Khalis

Ba'qubah

Mandali

Ar Ramadi

☆ **BAGHDAD**

IRAN

Badrah

Rutbah

Lake Ar-Razzazah

SOUTHERN NO-FLY ZONE

SMUGGLING ROUTES
Sanctions have done little to stem the flow of goods into Iraq, including banned components and dual-use equipment transported across the border with Jordan and through Iraq's port on the Persian Gulf

Al Hillah

Al Kut

Tigris River

Karbala

Ad Diwaniyah

An Najaf

Al 'Amarah

MOBILE LAUNCHERS
Experts believe Iraq is hiding Scud missiles on mobile launchers that cruise its western border to evade detection and lurk in range of Israeli and Saudi targets

Euphrates River

As Samawah

An Nasiriyah

Suq ash-Shuyukh

Basra

Known and Suspected Sites
- Nuclear weapons
- Chemical weapons
- Biological weapons
- Missiles
- Palaces

As-Salman

Al Faw

NOTE: Most of the information on Iraqi chemical-, biological- and nuclear-weapons production comes from intelligence gleaned from weapons inspections that essentially ended with the expulsion of UNSCOM inspectors in November 1998

SAUDI ARABIA

150 mi.

150 km

FACTORIES AND HOMES
Legitimate civilian projects such as a fertilizer plant can quickly and easily be diverted to produce material for chemical and biological weapons. Defectors say these are buried in residential basements

WELLS
According to a defector, Iraq built an extensive network of wells in rural areas, virtually undetectable by satellite, which are used to hide radioactive material and other compounds

KUWAIT

Persian Gulf

SMUGGLING

TIME Map by Joe Lertola
Text by Kathleen Adams

Sources: NASA, UNMOVIC, IAEA, Globalsecurity.org, Federation of American Scientists, Monterey Institute of International Studies, Iraq Watch

DOWNTOWN BAGHDAD

Army Canal

Saddam's Residence Palace of the Republic

Ministry of Defense

Former U.N. Inspectors' HQ

Al-Rashid Hotel

Military airport

Ministry of Information

Intelligence Service HQ

Tigris

New Palace

Baath Party HQ

Presidential Palace

American Embassy (closed)

SPACE IMAGING

3 mi.

3 km

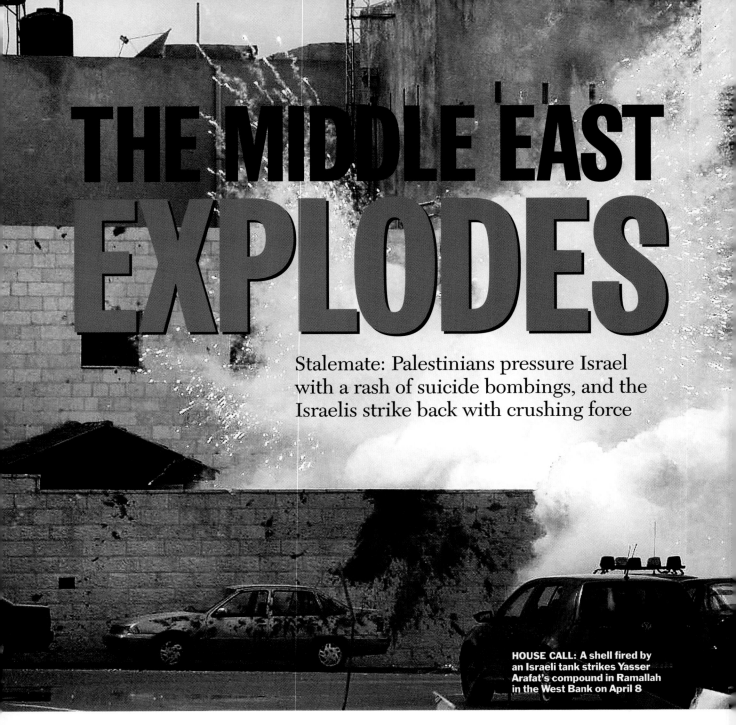

THE MIDDLE EAST EXPLODES

Stalemate: Palestinians pressure Israel with a rash of suicide bombings, and the Israelis strike back with crushing force

HOUSE CALL: A shell fired by an Israeli tank strikes Yasser Arafat's compound in Ramallah in the West Bank on April 8

IF CHARLES DICKENS WERE TO CHRONICLE THE YEAR 2002 in the Middle East, he might settle for one-half his familiar invocation from *A Tale of Two Cities:* "It was the worst of times … it was the age of foolishness … it was the season of darkness … it was the winter of despair." From the high point of optimism that surrounded the near miss Camp David talks in 2000, Israeli-Palestinian relations spiraled into an out-of-control melee of bloodletting in 2001, the only redeeming feature of which was that it obviously couldn't get any worse. In 2002 it got worse.

From the year's opening volley, a Jan. 9 Gaza Strip ambush in which four Israeli soldiers were killed, the Palestinians made it clear they intended to escalate the campaign of terror they began the previous year. As a result, they would take more Israeli lives in 2002 than in any previous year. And from the moment of Israel's reply two weeks later, which consisted of killing a Hamas commander with missiles fired from a helicopter, the Israelis made it clear they believed there was nothing to be gained by easing up on military retaliation. As a result—and as usual—twice as many Palestinians as Israelis would die during the year.

In 2002 both sides brought entirely new approaches to their long conflict. The Palestinians began relying on coordinated, simultaneous suicide-bomber attacks, designed to maximize the loss of civilian life, on a scale never before seen. Many of these attacks were followed by the broadcast of a videotape made a few hours beforehand, in which the suicide bomber extols the glories of martyrdom and

exhorts others to follow his (or, this year, for the first time, her) example. The appeals worked: the drumbeat of suicide bombings never seemed to let up. Only five times in the entire year did a full week pass without at least one attack.

In response to such horrors, the Israelis used to track and kill Palestinian terrorists with surgical air strikes or swift in-and-out raids. Although these techniques are still used, the Israelis this year began routinely occupying entire Palestinian cities for weeks at a time and blowing up or bulldozing buildings that reportedly housed wanted militants—not infrequently with people still alive inside. Israel

FACE-OFF: Locked in a spiral of death, Sharon and Arafat kept raising the stakes

also began to practice "targeted killings" (a euphemism for assassination) much more frequently.

But even Israel's overwhelming military strength could not make it invincible. Consider its experience in the Jenin camp, the West Bank Palestinian enclave that, in the decades since 1967, has taken on all the trappings of a permanent city. During house-to-house fighting in the alleyways of Jenin in April, Palestinian gunmen successfully ambushed and killed 13 Israeli soldiers—the worst loss of life for Israel's military in a single engagement in the entire 19 months of the current cycle of conflict. Ten more Israelis would die before the

JAN. 4
Israeli commandos board the freighter *Karine A.* in the Red Sea and find more than 50 tons of Iranian-made

JAN. 24
Israeli helicopter gunships fire two missiles into a car and kill senior Hamas military commander Bakr Hamdan. On the

FEB. 18
Saudi Arabia floats a peace plan: Israel to pull out of all occupied territories in exchange for peace with the Arab world. It soon dies

MARCH 27
A Passover suicide bombing at the Park Hotel in the coastal city of Netanya kills 29 people and wounds more than 100

weapons that are bound for the Gaza Strip. Five days later, Palestinian commandos ambush and kill four Israeli soldiers in the Gaza Strip

same day, four other Palestinians are killed in a series of other incidents in the Gaza Strip and the West bank town of Ramallah

MARCH 29
Ayat Akhras, 18, blows up a Jerusalem supermarket, killing two others and wounding more than 20. She is one of four women suicide bombers in 2002

MAYHEM: Andaleeb Taqatqa, a 20-year-old woman, set off a bomb in Jersalem on April 12 that killed six and wounded 80, only hours after Colin Powell met with Ariel Sharon in the city

army pulled out of Jenin several days later, and the Palestinians later claimed that the Israelis, in retaliation, had massacred hundreds of unarmed bystanders. Later reports by the United Nations and Human Rights Watch failed to confirm this charge, but found evidence that both sides had violated international law in the Jenin fighting.

As the cycle of Palestinian suicide bombings and deadly Israeli reprisals accelerated, the U.S. government kept its distance from the conflict, in line with President George Bush's criticism that the Clinton Administration had been too involved in attempts to broker peace between the antagonists. It was not until the late spring—while Israeli tanks were locking down the entire West Bank, dozens of Palestinian gunmen were holed up in Bethlehem's Church of the Nativity, and Palestinian Authority leader Yasser Arafat was besieged and isolated in his Ra-

mallah compound—that the White House began to take notice of the problem. Preoccupied by the war on terrorism, the Administration's foreign policy team seemed to realize all at once that if an outright war flared up in the area, it would derail its plans to build an international coalition against terrorists, if not spark an even larger conflict.

Within a matter of weeks, Secretary of State Colin Powell and U.S. envoy Anthony Zinni and CIA Director George Tenet were in the region, trying to jump-start negotiations. Their efforts quickly bore fruit: they succeeded in ending the Nativity siege, getting Arafat sprung from Ramallah and temporarily rolling back Israel's military occupation of the West Bank. But even such real achievements seemed like a bandage on a hemorrhage. After a three-week respite in June, the suicide bombings started up again and both sides sank further into a numbed moral exhaustion that robbed them of the energy needed for any-

MAY 2
Yasser Arafat emerges from 34 days of being confined by Israeli troops in his office compound in Ramallah

MAY 10
After a five-week siege, some 240 Palestinians file out of the Church of the Nativity in Bethlehem. The standoff

JUNE 6
Hours after a huge suicide car bomb explodes next to a crowded bus in the northern town of Megiddo, killing 17, Israeli forces again lay siege to Arafat's

APRIL 12
Israeli troops withdraw from the Jenin refugee camp after fighting claims dozens of lives on both sides. Palestinians accuse Israel of a massacre, but the U.N. blames both sides

ended with a deal that transferred 26 wanted Palestinians to internal exile in Gaza and sent 13 militants abroad to various European countries

MAY 19
A suicide bomber disguised in an Israeli army uniform blows himself up in a Netanya outdoor marketplace, killing four people and wounding more than 60

Ramallah compound, trapping him for nine days. At this time, Ariel Sharon visits the U.S. and meets with George Bush. Only days after Arafat's siege is lifted, a suicide bomb in Jerusalem kills 19 people

thing but continuing the deadly, stalemated exchange of punch and counterpunch.

The Bush team was frustrated by the intransigence of both sides. In the spring, Colin Powell had publicly scolded Ariel Sharon's government, saying, "[If you] think you can solve the problem by seeing how many Palestinians can be killed—I don't know if that leads you anywhere." Within days, the White House demanded that Israeli forces pull back from areas supposed to be under Palestinian control and that Arafat act to stop Palestinian terror attacks. Israeli forces did temporarily pull back, but the Palestinian attacks went on. By July, Bush was publicly agreeing with Sharon that Arafat must go.

By summer's end, Arafat's compound would be surrounded three more times; every major city, town and refugee camp in the West Bank would once again be occupied; negotiations would founder; and hundreds more people would die on both sides. Meanwhile, the hard-core Israeli settler movement continued to grab new land in the midst of heavily populated Palestinian areas. In 2002 alone, settlers started dozens of new settlements, daring Sharon's government not to protect them. Once, both Israeli and Palestinian investigators later agreed, radical settlers resorted to terror of their own, planting two bombs in a Palestinian school and injuring five children.

The battle over the new settlements led to the fall of Sharon's coalition government at the end of October, when the opposition Labor Party balked at a $145 million subsidy that Sharon's Likud Party had slated for the settlers. The only way Sharon could continue to govern was to invite his Likud archrival, Benjamin Netanyahu, to join the government. Netanyahu has vied with Sharon for years over which of them takes a harder line with the Palestinians. He agreed to serve, but with a price: he demanded elections in January, in which he hoped to become P.M.

Arafat has similar troubles. The Palestinian parliament, furious over his corrupt administration, delivered a vote of no confidence

in September and forced his entire 21-member Cabinet to resign. Palestinian moderates are disenchanted with Arafat's inability to break the deadlock, while radical factions have concluded that he is useless and are preparing to continue the struggle after he is driven into exile (as Sharon has repeatedly threatened) or killed (as militant Palestinians have repeatedly threatened). And Arafat faces a Palestinian presidential election, also scheduled for January.

Amid political uncertainty on both sides, the U.S. presented a new "road map" in October that envisions Palestinian statehood no later than 2005. But amid the furor, the directions to peace seemed impossible to plot. On election day, Nov. 28, two Palestinian gunmen sprayed a Likud polling place with machine gun fire, killing six people. Later that day, Sharon beat Netanyahu handily in the Likud primary, which means he will face Labor's new leader, Amram Mitzna, in a general election on January 28.

But the day's worst news came from Kenya, not the Middle East. The strikes against Israelis in Mombasa [see p. 35] signalled two ominous developments—the introduction of anti-Israeli violence outside the Jewish state's borders and the possible entry of al-Qaeda into the campaign of terror against Israel. Sharon began his speech accepting Likud's nomination with a moment of silence for the dead. It was one of the few such moments in the region this year. ∎

JAMAL ARURI—AFP

BLOOD! In March, Israeli students wave paint-stained hands as they protest a proposed lecture by a Palestinian leader in Jerusalem

JUNE 27
Israeli helicopters fire four missiles into a Palestinian Authority compound in Hebron, where more than a

JULY 17
One day after nine Israelis are killed in a West Bank ambush, a suicide bombing in Tel Aviv kills three and wounds more than 40

JULY 23
An Israeli F-16 jet drops a one-ton bomb on a Gaza City apartment building, killing Hamas leader Salah Shehadeh,

NOV. 28
Ariel Sharon beats Benjamin Netanyahu, left, in the Likud party primary and will face Labor's new leader, Amram Mitzna, in a Jan. 28 election

dozen fugitives are holed up. After a four-day siege, the Palestinian gunmen refuse to come out of the Hebron fortress, and the Israeli army reduces it to rubble

AMERICAN RED CROSS

his bodyguard and 13 bystanders. The death toll includes Shehadeh's wife, his daughter, and eight other children

OCT. 21
A suicide bomb in the northern Israeli town of Hadera kills 16 people, one day before a top-ranking U.S. diplomat is due to arrive in Israel for new peace talks

AT WAR WITH WATER

Massive floods rampage across Europe, leaving chaos in their wake

AUGUST 2002: THE CITIZENS OF PRAGUE PREPARE FOR war. As sirens wail, volunteers build sandbag barricades and rescue workers go door to door evacuating residents and tourists. Museum curators scurry to secure paintings, rare manuscripts and other precious objects, while appeals for donations of blood, food and clothing are broadcast over radio and television. Military rescue vehicles take up positions across the city.

The residents of Prague were at war with the elements, as a week of heavy rains swelled the Vltava River to 35 times its average flow, swamping the metro system, collapsing apartment buildings and displacing some 50,000 people. It was the worst flood to hit Prague in more than a century. But when the waters receded, the city could claim a major victory. Thanks to a hastily built, 1.2-mile-long mobile floodwall, the historic Old Town—home to such treasures as the Old Town Square, the 15th century Astronomical Clock and the famous Jewish quarter—was largely spared.

Other parts of Europe were not so lucky, as torrential downpours sent floodwaters raging from the Baltic to the Black Sea, killing at least 100 people and causing billions of dollars' worth of damage to buildings, infrastructure

VENICE ON THE VLTAVA:
The swollen river invades the UNESCO-protected historic town of Cesky Krumlov in the Czech Republic

HELP ON THE WAY: Rescue workers at the Prague Zoo, top, evacuate a rhinoceros in a sling as Vltava River waters descend on the Old City. In the center picture, a man pilots a homemade raft in the flooded streets of Meissen, near Dresden, eastern Germany, where avenues became canals. At bottom, inhabitants of the eastern German city of Grimma, near Leipzig, are lifted out of their homes to safety by a front-end loader.

and crops. Austria's capital, Vienna, was largely spared when a 12-mile-long canal was constructed parallel to the Danube to drain floodwaters. But in lower Austria, the Danube broke through dikes near Ybbs, trapping more than 3,000 of the town's 5,800 residents in their homes.

Germany wasn't spared: at Dresden's Zwinger Palace, home to one of Europe's greatest collections of Baroque and Renaissance art, hundreds of people worked partly by candlelight to move thousands of objects to higher levels as water flooded the cellars and other storage areas. Huge floods in Russia caused by far the most deaths—as many as 100—but garnered the least international attention.

The residents of Prague have certainly learned their lesson. A barrier similar to the mobile floodwall that was assembled around the Old Town's perimeter had also been planned for the Mala Strana district, which was severely damaged. But 18 months of bureaucratic wrangling delayed its completion. Delay is no longer an option. ∎

GOD SAVE THE QUEEN

Toasting the Queen's jubilee, Britain parades on her reign

A PARTY FIT FOR A QUEEN? NOW THAT'S A CHALLENGE. Staging festivities to mark Queen Elizabeth II's 50 years on the throne offered the British royal family a much-needed opportunity to mend fences with its subjects. The climb back from Princess Diana's death in 1997, when the Queen's wooden initial response provoked public fury, had been arduous. Unfortunately, the deaths early in the year of both the Queen's mother and sister, Princess Margaret, promised to put a damper on things.

Not to worry. The crowds greeting the monarch in her jubilee tours of the country were big and kind: 20,000 in Falmouth, 30,000 in Newcastle. Slowly, the truth dawned: the crowds were turning out to show respect for a dutiful woman who had fulfilled every task expected of her, day after day, for 50 years. In short … long live the Queen!

Over the four-day jubilee weekend, Elizabeth II drove in her gilded state coach through a massive throng to a thanksgiving service at St. Paul's Cathedral. She presided over a lengthy parade that included a Hell's Angels biker, a 5,000-person gospel choir and bevies of prancing minions from faraway Commonwealth lands.

And that was just in the daytime. The Queen also opened the gates of Buckingham Palace for a two-night "Party at the Palace." The first night was a concert of classical music; the second was an all-star revue of British pop music of the second Elizabethan era, beginning with Queen guitarist Brian May thrashing out *God Save the Queen* from a perch atop the palace and ending with a mass singalong of *All You Need Is Love* led by Sir Paul McCartney. In between, a *Who's Who* of five decades of British pop paraded across the stage—from Cliff Richard to Eric Clapton to, yes, Ozzy Osbourne. "I said to Her Majesty, 'Are we going to do this again next year?'" McCartney told the crowd. "And she said, 'Not on my lawn.'"

And so to bed. Alas, this story—like the monarchy—must go on. Come fall, the royals were back in the tattle again. Princess Diana's former butler Paul Burrell came forward with a titillating stream of revelations: he had sneaked Diana's lovers into Kensington Palace in the trunk of his car; Diana had once greeted her lover Hasnat Khan wearing only a fur coat and jewels. Tales from other sources—none of them corroborated—told of an aide to Prince Charles having raping the Prince's male valet, of gay orgies aboard the royal yacht … and on and on. Sadly, the good vibes of the jubilee seemed to have been only a summer fling. ∎

POSH TO POP: Clockwise from top, the Queen, 76, and Prince Philip, 81, salute their subjects. The Union Jack was de rigueur. A scrum of princes forms at St. Paul's Cathedral: from left, William, Edward, Harry and Charles. Pensioners on scooters liven up the big parade, and Queen guitarist Brian May opens the pop concert from a lofty perch.

Reporters of Light

An international gallery by TIME photographers

Photograph for TIME by James Nachtwey—VII

KABUL, AFGHANISTAN
A teacher exhorts his students in an art class at Habibia High School. Among its pupils are girls who were barred from education under the Taliban. The classroom bears the scars of its front-line position in the Afghan civil war, but it is actually enviable: in many worse-off areas, students attend class outdoors.

KABUL, AFGHANISTAN
Voting with their feet for a social revolution, Afghan women dressed up for a wedding party dare to go bare—partially—allowing their high heels to show beneath their finery. Such an ostentatious display of luxury (and sexuality) would have been a serious crime under the mullahs' rule.

Carrying on the work pioneered by such notable figures as Robert Capa, W. Eugene Smith and Alfred Eisenstaedt, photographers James Nachtwey, Christopher Morris, Alexandra Boulat and John Stanmeyer criss-cross the world for TIME, returning with images that illuminate cultures and put a human face on dull statistics. Illuminate is the key word here: these are journalists who use different tools than their colleagues but to the same end. As the term photojournalism implies, they are reporters of light.

Yes, it can be dangerous work. Morris was taken captive by Iraqi troops during the Gulf War in 1991 and held in Baghdad, where he was frantically shuttled among sealed rooms for six days before being released to allied forces. Nachtwey has been reported dead in Sri Lanka and shot at in Bosnia. In South Africa, a bullet parted his hair as he tried to rescue a fatally wounded colleague. "Don't call me a war photographer," he says. "I'm an antiwar photographer. If war is an attempt to negate humanity, then photography can be perceived as the opposite of war."

Photograph for TIME by Alexandra Boulat—VII

Photograph for TIME by James Stanmeyer—VII

HERAT, AFGHANISTAN
Enjoying the fruits of freedom, followers of Sufism enter a trance during prayer at a shrine. Branded deviants by the Taliban, Sufis were forbidden to practice their rites, which employ music and dance to induce a mystical state. Other religious minorities, like Hindus and Sikhs, were also forbidden to practice their religion.

NABLUS, WEST BANK
An Israeli tank guards the ruins of the ancient Casbah in Nablus as Palestinians look out from their damaged home onto the devastation left by Israeli forces. After weeks of mounting terror in Israel in the face of Palestinian suicide bombings, Israeli troops mounted a military incursion into West Bank areas in search of militants.

KABUL, AFGHANISTAN
U.S. special-forces trainers do their best to instill a gung-ho spirit in recruits for the Afghan national army. A strong centralized force will be essential as new President Hamid Karzai attempts to bring unity to a land riven by tribalism and formerly ruled by local warlords. The U.S. and France hope to build a 60,000-man force within five years.

Photograph for TIME by James Nachtwey—VII

Photograph for TIME by Christopher Morris—VII

Photograph for TIME by Alexandra Boulat—VII

KABUL, AFGHANISTAN
Celebrating life in the precincts of death,
an Afghan boy swings from a tree over graves
in a cemetery. He is fortunate. Extreme
poverty (an estimated 70% of the population
is malnourished) forces many parents to send
their children out to work at an early age.

SOLO, INDONESIA
Flexing his muscles, a student sports a shirt bearing
his hero's image as he lifts weights at the *madrasah*
(Islamic school) run by Muslim cleric Abubakar Ba'asyir,
head of the radical Mujahidin Council of Indonesia and
suspected leader of Jemaah Islamiah, a network of
terrorist cells in Southeast Asia.

Photograph for TIME by James Nachtwey—VII

Profile

A Dutch Rebel Is Slain

Pim Fortuyn broke the mold for politicians, even in the famously tolerant Netherlands. The onetime professor and newsmagazine columnist traveled in a Daimler with a fender flag bearing the family crest, employed a butler, wore tailored Italian suits and reveled in his homosexuality. He became involved in electoral politics in 2001—and

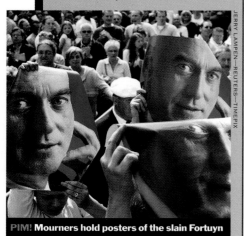

PIM! Mourners hold posters of the slain Fortuyn

soon made waves by declaring Islam a "backward culture" and advocating the repeal of Holland's laws forbidding religious and racial discrimination. Running for Parliament on an anti-immigration platform in a May election, the controversial right-winger was expected to win enough votes to make him a major player in forming Holland's new government.

As Fortuyn left a radio studio after an interview, a gunman approached him and fired five shots. Fortuyn died soon after. The shooter was apprehended: Volkert van der Graaf, 33, an animal-rights and environmental activist.

In death, Fortuyn became a martyr: the man who had been widely branded a racist took on the luster of his avowed idol, John F. Kennedy. In the election, his party gained 26 seats in Parliament and became part of a briefly-serving coalition government. The events reflected a trend in Europe: moderate-right parties are rising, as moderate-left groups are fading.

MEMORIES A widow of a Milosevic victim reacts to the trial

A Fool for a Client?

Slobodan Milosevic, the former President of Yugoslavia, stands trial before an international tribunal in the Hague, accused of genocide and war crimes in the bloody strife in the Balkans in the 1990s. Milosevic, 61, a former law student, acted as his own lawyer in the trial, which began in February. Though he claimed not to recognize the court's jurisdiction, Milosevic participated vigorously in the proceedings, probing witnesses for flaws in their testimony and often prolonging the sessions with political rants or by raising points of order. His stalling tactics were working: angry prosecutors said they might not be able to present their case in fully damning detail. The trial is now expected to last until 2004. By August, the prosecutors had already backed off their goal of convicting Milosevic of genocide against the Bosnian Croats, part of their initial charges.

The Restless Subcontinent

Long-simmering enmity between Hindu India and Muslim Pakistan, both now nuclear powers, came

Roundup

South America in Turmoil

With their economies in a deep slump, South Americans turned against what they described as U.S. economic hegemony: Argentines rioted repeatedly, and Brazilians voted in a leftist President who criticized American policies. In Venezuela, Hugo Chávez barely clung to power.

BRAZIL: In a landslide vote, Luiz Lula da Silva, a former factory worker and labor leader, was elected Brazil's first left-leaning President in almost 40 years

ARGENTINA: Striking protesters burn a U.S. flag in May. Argentines view the International Monetary Fund as a tool of U.S. power and blame the IMF for their woes

VENEZUELA: Embattled President Hugo Chávez survived a general strike and abortive coup in April but faced an even larger general strike in December

STANDOFF Vajpayee and Musharraf

close to flaring into war in 2002.

The issue, once again, was Kashmir. On the Indian side of the partitioned region's Line of Control, Kashmir has a Muslim majority, fueling Pakistan's claim to the territory. But India refuses to let it go. May 14 suicide strikes by three suspected Pakistani militants in the city of Jammu killed 31 people and sparked a new crisis. Coming in the wake of deadly February riots in Gujarat, the May episode saw the two sides mobilize a total of 1 million troops in front-line positions.

Pakistan's President Pervez Musharraf was in the hottest seat. Already denounced by extremist Muslims for his

support of the U.S. war on terror, the former general alienated middle-class Pakistanis by holding a rigged referendum on his rule in April. Musharraf and Indian President A.B. Vajpayee escaped the crisis without war—this time.

China: Hu's in Charge?

Meeting in Beijing in November, China's ruling Communist Party anointed a new generation of leaders in a tightly scripted convocation with a surprise ending. As expected, the nation's new head man will be little-known party functionary Hu Jintao, 59. But the old boss, Jiang

Zemin, 76, due to resign, remained in command of China's military and has retained allies in many top positions. Some fear

JINTAO Figurehead?

China is in for a period of political infighting—a recipe for stasis.

A Tanker Tragedy off Spain

After the *Prestige*, an oil tanker bearing 77,000 tons of fuel, ruptured its hull in rough seas off

LAST MOMENTS The *Prestige* broke in two, then went down

Spain's Galicia coast, 24 crew members were airlifted to safety. The captain was arrested when he refused to allow the ship to be towed, and then the damaged vessel was tugged 150 miles out to sea, where it broke apart and sank. The oil spill was nearly twice as big as that of the 1989 *Exxon Valdez* spill in Alaska. Experts said it would take months to assess the full extent of the damage.

Photograph by Carl Seibert—SF *Sun-Sentinel*—Corbis Sygma

For Buccaneers of the Bottom Line, There's No Place Like Home

In Boca Raton did Sullivan a stately pleasure-dome decree … and normally, no one except the neighbors would have noticed. But in a year forever tarnished by corporate chicanery, the $15 million Florida mansion being constructed by Scott Sullivan, 40, the former CFO of telecom giant WorldCom, became the poster palace of executive excess. Let's run the numbers. Cost of land: $2.5 million. Square footage: 17,000. Windows: 117. Interior doors: 98. Seats in private movie theater: 18. Corinthian columns: 13. Refrigerators: 9. Jacuzzis: 6. Guest suites: 4. Fur-storage rooms: 1 (well, you have to skimp somewhere).

Name: **Dennis Kozlowski**
Company: **Tyco**
Arraigned: **Sept. 12, 2002**

Name: **Scott Sullivan**
Company: **WorldCom**
Arraigned: **March 9, 2002**

YEAR OF THE PERP WALK

Corrupt executives cost investors billions and tarnish American business

Name: **Andrew Fastow**
Company: **Enron**
Arraigned: **Oct. 2, 2002**

Name: **Sam Waksal**
Company: **ImClone**
Arraigned: **June 12, 2002**

H OW TO CALCULATE THE TOTAL LOSSES caused by the U.S. business scandals of 2002? Forget the millions of dollars looted outright by crooked executives: it's peanuts. Consider the billions in savings lost by the employees of bankrupt companies—in many cases a lifetime's nest egg, held in company stock. Now add in the billions lost by the investing public—the total shareholder equity that simply evaporated when stocks inflated by lies collapsed. But the most significant toll is the hardest to quantify: the deficit we now run in our confidence in American companies—and in the brokerage houses, accounting firms and federal regulatory agencies that failed to monitor them. Pick your price tag. But whichever method of calculation you choose, the total of what we've lost comes to far more than we can afford.

ENRON

CEO: Kenneth Lay
Alleged M.O.: Fake the books, fool the regulators
Bottom Line: $67 billion in equity lost

T HE FALL OF ENERGY GIANT ENRON, ONCE RANKED seventh on the FORTUNE 500 list, began with a trickle of revelations in the autumn of 2001 related to misconduct at the firm's outside auditor, accounting firm Arthur Andersen. But this trickle quickly turned into an unstoppable flood when, on Oct. 16, 2001, Enron predicted that, rather than making a profit for the year (as investors and government regulators had been led to expect), it would run up a loss of $618 million. A worse revelation followed: Enron had lost more than $1 billion over the previous five years—while it had claimed to be making a profit. Not everyone was crooked: vice president Sherron Watkins warned CEO Kenneth Lay in an August, 2001, memo that the books looked shady. She was ignored.

The company filed for bankruptcy protection on Dec. 2. In short order, the stock price fell from the low 80s to just pennies, $67 billion in shareholder equity was wiped out, and $1 billion of the retirement savings of Enron employees (largely in company stock) had evaporated. A shattered Arthur Andersen quit the auditing business in August.

How does a company hide billions of dollars in losses and debt from accountants, regulators, investors, bankers, and the media? Good question. Some critics have blamed a too cozy relationship between Enron and its rightful watchdogs: Andersen accountants who didn't want to make waves that might disrupt the flow of millions of dollars in consulting fees; regulators who may have been

Kenneth Lay

Andrew Fastow

David Duncan

Sherron Watkins

daunted by Enron's chummy status with the Bush Administration (CEO Lay was a personal friend of the President's and a major contributor to his campaign); and stock analysts who may have gone easy on Enron, lest they endanger their own companies' investment banking fees.

Congress was eager to examine these issues in February, but a parade of half a dozen Enron executives, led by Lay, invoked the Fifth Amendment and refused to answer any questions. This left the matter in the hands of prosecutors, who began to probe from the outer edges of the Enron fiscal labyrinth to the center.

A chorus of pleas followed. In April, David Duncan, the top Enron auditor at Andersen, pleaded guilty to obstruction of justice and turned government informant. In August, Michael Kopper, the former head of Enron's global finance unit, pleaded guilty to conspiracy to commit wire fraud and money laundering. In October, energy trader Timothy Belden pleaded guilty to wire fraud for his role in manipulating electricity prices during California's energy crisis in the years 2000 and 2001. On Oct. 31 Andrew Fastow, Enron's former chief financial officer, was indicted on 78 counts of fraud, money laundering, conspiracy, obstruction of justice and other charges. Fastow has pleaded innocent and is awaiting trial—but the drive to bring the shoddy house of Enron to justice isn't likely to stop with him.

John Rigas

ADELPHIA

CEO: John Rigas
Alleged M.O.: Hide family debt on company books
Bottom Line: $60 billion in equity lost

FOUNDER JOHN RIGAS AND HIS SONS MICHAEL, TIMOTHY and James built Adelphia into the sixth largest cable-television operation in America. Now it seems the Rigas family had been treating Adelphia the same way they treated the Pennsylvania movie theater that gave John Rigas his start—as a small-town family business with an open till. The trouble began with the revelation in March that the Rigases had borrowed $2.3 billion through family-owned partnerships and that the debt had been kept off Adlephia's balance sheet.

Michael Rigas

By June, a perfect storm had broken. The SEC and two federal grand juries were investigating Adelphia's books, its stock was trading for pennies and was delisted from NASDAQ. Rigas and his sons had given up their Adelphia director-ships, leaving the company liable for some $3 billion in Rigas-family debts.

Where did all the money go? Adelphia's new management found the family had used the company's cash and assets to buy a professional hockey team, a golf course, thousands of acres of timberland, a furniture company, a car dealership and other cable-TV systems—without the approval of the company's board.

On July 24, federal agents arrested John, Timothy and Michael Rigas, as well as two other Adelphia managers; the SEC filed a civil suit against the company and its executives. By the end of September, formal indictments were handed up against Rigas and his two sons for conspiracy, securities fraud and wire fraud. Their trial may not begin until late 2003. The trials of Adelphia stockholders are ongoing: they lost $60 billion in equity in 2002.

IMCLONE

CEO: Sam Waksal
Alleged M.O.: Beat stock dive with insider info
Bottom Line: Martha Stewart loses $300 million

THE TIMING WAS, TO BE KIND ABOUT IT, FISHY. ON DEC. 28, 2001, the FDA rejected an application by drug-maker ImClone for fast-track approval of its cancer-fighting drug, Erbitux. Then it turned out that just 24 hours before the decision was announced, both Aliza Waksal, daughter of ImClone founder and CEO Samuel Waksal, and gracious-living doyen Martha Stewart (a close friend of Waksal's) had each dumped thousands of shares of ImClone stock. And they weren't alone: ImClone officers and directors, as well as other members of Waksal's family, had sold more than $70 million worth of the company's stock in the weeks before the FDA announcement.

Sam Waksal

By May, Waksal had resigned as ImClone's CEO. The next month he was being investigated by the House Energy and Commerce Committee, which also announced it was looking into Stewart's sale of the stock.

Waksal was arrested on June 12, charged with trading illegally on insider information. At this point, Stewart issued a statement that her Im-Clone stock had been sold on the basis of a prior agreement with her Merrill Lynch broker, Peter Bacanovic, and his assistant, Douglas Faneuil, to divest if the share price dipped below $60. The pair initially backed Stewart's story; still, Merrill Lynch suspended them.

In September the Justice Department began a criminal probe of Stewart. In October, Faneuil began cooperating with prosecutors—and Stewart resigned from the board of the New York Stock Exchange. On Oct. 15, Waksal pleaded guilty to six counts of securities fraud, perjury, obstruction of justice, conspiracy and bank fraud—but not to seven other charges that would have incriminated Stewart or his family. Weeks later, the SEC notified Stewart that it would file civil fraud charges against her. By mid-November, shares of Stewart's stock were down 65%, and her personal fortune had shrunk more than $300 million. All because of a stock trade that saved her less than $240,000.

Douglas Faneuil   Martha Stewart

Bernard Ebbers

WORLDCOM

CEO: **Bernard Ebbers**
Alleged M.O.: **Fix books so costs are investments**
Bottom Line: **The biggest bankruptcy in history**

TELECOMMUNICATIONS COLOSSUS WORLDCOM RODE the 1990s boom like a rocket, its growth fueled by acquisitions and funded by a stock price that, year after year, just kept ascending. But the stock peaked in June 1999 and was faltering by early 2002: both growth and cash flow ground to a halt, while debt kept piling up. When massive layoffs in February 2002 failed to kick-start earnings or boost the stock price, WorldCom's bankers demanded a fresh look at the company's books.

Scott Sullivan

What they found was disturbing: WorldCom had lent its founder and CEO, Bernard Ebbers, more than $400 million. The board of directors (which hadn't known about these loans) forced Ebbers to resign, but auditors also found that WorldCom had been improperly booking operating expenses as capital expenditures, a classic form of accounting fraud. On July 8, Ebbers and CFO Scott Sullivan invoked the Fifth Amendment, refusing to testify before Congress.

WorldCom's ride was over: the stock price plummeted from a high of more than $64 to less than $1, and the company was forced to file the largest bankruptcy petition in U.S. history. In August, Sullivan and controller David Myers were arrested on charges including securities fraud and conspiracy. By October, Myers had pleaded guilty and agreed to testify against Sullivan. The former CFO has pleaded not guilty and awaits trial in 2003. WorldCom's kingpin, Ebbers, had not been charged with any wrongdoing by mid-November, but federal prosecutors assured the public that more indictments were forthcoming.

TYCO

CEO: **Dennis Kozlowski**
Alleged M.O.: **Cook the books, buy toys for boss**
Bottom Line: **$8 billion in undisclosed deals**

TYCO CEO DENNIS KOZLOWSKI COBBLED TOGETHER A patchwork of acquisitions (in businesses ranging from financial services to medical supplies to telecommunications and electronic security) that transformed the manufacturing company into a billion-dollar conglomerate and its CEO into one of America's best-paid executives. Kozlowski pulled down $19 million in cash and almost $80 million in stock from 1998 through 2001. But when Tyco's explosive growth began to slow, Kozlowski announced a bold plan in January 2002: he would split the company into four parts, sell some units and spin others off. But one corporate suitor after another walked away from any deal after perusing Tyco's books.

The public caught the first whiff of trouble in February, when chief financial officer Mark Swartz revealed that Tyco had spent $8 billion in the past three fiscal years on 700 acquisitions that were never disclosed, some of which had been used to inflate Tyco's cash flow artificially. The market's reaction was punishing: Tyco's shares lost almost one-third of their value.

Outside auditors soon found strange expenditures on Tyco's books: $15,000 for an umbrella stand, $6,000 for a shower curtain, $2,900 for coat hangers. The items graced an $18 million New York City apartment that Tyco had bought for Kozlowski. Theoretically, the Tyco CEO would be using it when he wasn't in the $19 million mansion in Boca Raton, Fla., or the $6 million ocean-front home on Nantucket Island, Mass., that Tyco had bought for him. All told, the SEC would eventually allege, Kozlowski improperly used $242 million in Tyco funds to pay for yachts, fine art, jewelry and luxury homes.

While Kozlowski enjoyed the $13 million in artworks Tyco bought in his name, he forgot to pay sales taxes on them. In June, New York State prosecutors indicted him on charges of evading more than $1 million in such taxes. Kozlowski resigned his position one day before the indictment was made public. In a separate, September indictment, Kozlowski and two other former Tyco executives were charged with operating Tyco as a "criminal enterprise" to defraud investors, citing tens of millions of dollars in loans that were never repaid. In November a judge set a trial date of June 2003 for Kozlowski, who said he would spend the 2002 holidays at his 17-room mansion in Vail, Colo.—not to be confused with the Vale of Tears. ■

Dennis Kozlowski

BIG, BUT THRIFTY: Ford says this new hybrid Explorer SUV will get up to 40 m.p.g. The fuel-stingy behemoth should hit showrooms in 2003.

NOT YOUR DADDY'S SUV

After a few false starts, a new breed of hybrid cars hits the road

WE EXPECT OUR MOVIE STARS TO DRIVE SLEEK, high-end automobiles. So why have both Cameron Diaz's Porsche and her Mercedes-Benz been gathering dust in her garage for months? Because these days the stylish actress tools around Tinseltown in a $20,000 Toyota Prius—a hybrid car that swings both ways, alternately guzzling climate-heating gasoline and sipping environmentally friendly electricity. What the car lacks in class it makes up in fuel savings and reduced emissions. "I love my Prius," says Diaz, 29, who reports that the batteries on her luxury cars have both died from neglect. "The Prius is all I drive."

Bill Maher, former host of *Politically Incorrect*, also drives a hybrid car. Leonardo DiCaprio likes his hybrid so much that he bought three more, for his mom, dad and stepmom—and took time out from a Steven Spielberg set to boast to TIME about his new wheels. "People are always impressed," he notes, "with the way it drives, the gas mileage and how quiet it is."

If celebrity endorsements sold cars, hybrids would be flying off dealers' lots. But with their oddball designs, the

Acceleration

The **BATTERY-POWERED MOTOR** provides extra power for faster acceleration

Cruising

When the **GAS ENGINE** is running on its own, it also recharges the **BATTERY** via the electric motor

Braking

Kinetic energy from the moving car is converted into electric energy, which is stored in the **BATTERY**

first generation of hybrids barely dented the consciousness of car-buying Americans. According to one survey, most Americans still think the batteries in hybrids have to be plugged in to recharge. (Wrong. They are rejuiced automatically as you drive.) No wonder only 20,000 of the 17 million automobiles sold in the U.S. in 2001 were hybrids.

But now the auto industry is taking another crack at it. A hybrid version of the Honda Civic, the best-selling compact car in America, started rolling into dealerships nationwide in April, 2002. Ford, which has produced a string of electric cars, is expected to be the first U.S. manufacturer to introduce a hybrid vehicle, in 2003. Meanwhile, Toyota, General Motors and Chrysler have all promised a new crop of hybrid vehicles by 2004.

Despite the excitement, hybrids still have a major hurdle to overcome: sticker shock (more on that later). But for car buyers who want to do their part for the environment and are willing pay a few grand extra to do it, hybrids are the only game in Motown. So ... hop in.

The first thing you notice when you drive one is how quiet it is. The engine goes blissfully silent every time you stop at an intersection. That's because the gas engine shuts off to allow the electric motor to take over. Gas engines are at their least efficient—and produce the most emissions—when idling, so that's when it makes the most sense to make the switch. The cars are chock-full of clever tricks like this. Every time you touch the brakes, kinetic energy that would normally be lost in the braking system is recaptured by the electric motor, which in turn recharges the battery. The process is known as regenerative braking. Some hybrids use their electric motors to control the power steering or to give the car extra oomph at higher speeds.

Hybrids are surprisingly fun to drive. The electric motor on the Toyota Prius can keep the car cruising at speeds up to 42 m.p.h. without any help, although it needs power from the gas engine to accelerate to that speed. A panel on the dashboard displays average fuel efficiency, calculated on the fly, and tells you when the electric motor is being used to charge the batteries or assist the gas engine.

The new hybrid Civic uses a smaller electric motor and a more powerful gas engine than the Prius, so it's always burning gas, except when it's braking or standing still. Even so, it gets 47 m.p.g. in the city and 51 m.p.g. on the freeway, a 25% improvement over the gas-only version. Aside from a small hybrid logo on the trunk, it looks like a regular Civic. About the only drawbacks are the higher sticker price (it's roughly $2,500 more than a similarly equipped standard Civic) and slightly slower acceleration.

Ford, for its part, claims that when its hybrid Escape SUV goes on sale, it will have all the zip of the regular Escape, even though it will run off a smaller four-cylinder engine. The extra horsepower is supposed to come from a state-of-the-art electric motor. The company is promising an impressive 40 m.p.g. in city driving, vs. the 23 m.p.g. the gas-only version gets today.

TIME writer Anita Hamilton has driven a futuristic Ford lately. Her report: "I got behind the wheel of a hybrid Escape when I visited Ford's product-development center in Dearborn, Mich., in April, 2002. Ford would not let me drive the prototype up the steepest test hills or around the

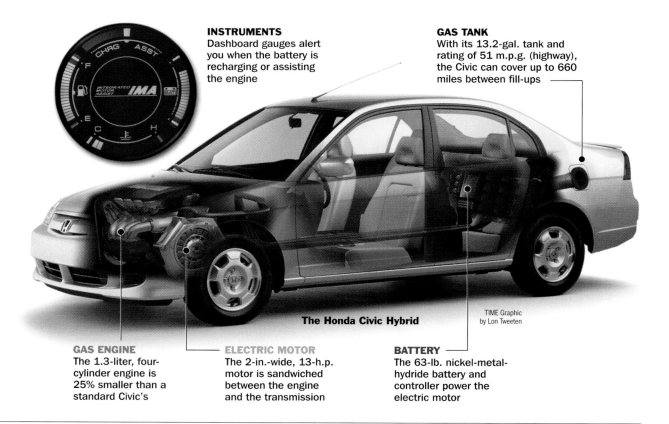

INSTRUMENTS
Dashboard gauges alert you when the battery is recharging or assisting the engine

GAS TANK
With its 13.2-gal. tank and rating of 51 m.p.g. (highway), the Civic can cover up to 660 miles between fill-ups

The Honda Civic Hybrid

TIME Graphic
by Lon Tweeten

GAS ENGINE
The 1.3-liter, four-cylinder engine is 25% smaller than a standard Civic's

ELECTRIC MOTOR
The 2-in.-wide, 13-h.p. motor is sandwiched between the engine and the transmission

BATTERY
The 63-lb. nickel-metal-hydride battery and controller power the electric motor

sharpest curves, but I was impressed by the gentle, seamless shifting between the gas engine and electric power at low speeds. The car went silent every time I released the gas pedal or drove it slowly in reverse."

For all their benefits, however, hybrids do cost a few thousand dollars more than their gas-only counterparts. Whereas you may be able to recoup that money in fuel savings within 10 years, it's still a big initial investment. And the batteries are guaranteed under warranty for only eight years, at which point customers may have to shell out as much as $2,000 for a replacement. "People are not willing to pay extra money for fuel economy in the U.S.," says Rich Marsh, who heads GM's hybrid-truck program. That's why GM plans to market its hybrid GMC Sierra and Chevrolet Silverado pickups, due out in 2004, not on their tiny 2-m.p.g. improvement in fuel consumption but on the benefits of their onboard electric generators and standard outlets for plugging in power tools.

It's still hard to tell whether Detroit is really serious about the hybrid-car business. After all, the same companies touting their hybrids today also lobbied successfully to put the brakes on legislation that would have mandated tougher fuel-efficiency standards. President Bush has proposed tax credits of $2,000 to $3,000 for hybrid-car buyers, but those funds aren't likely to kick in until 2004, if ever. Until then, if you want your fancy hybrid car, you'll have to pay a premium. Maybe it's the snob factor that makes hybrids a hit in Beverly Hills. ■

GOING TOPLESS: THE RAGTOPS RETURN

They're back! Nearly extinct a few years ago, convertibles are the latest rage among car buyers. Today the market is flooded with 30 convertibles, up from about a dozen six years ago. The new fleet ranges from family-oriented cruisers like the Toyota Camry Solara to such trophy hot rods as the Lexus SC 430. Even Chevy's pickup division is joining the fray, with a "sport roadster" set to roll into showrooms in 2003.

What accounts for the sudden revival of convertibles? Automakers seem to have rediscovered a couple of old maxims units when it introduced the vehicle in 2000, charging about $5,000 more than for the comparable hardtop. Now Chrysler and Volkswagen are racing to produce convertible derivatives to bolster slowing sales of the PT Cruiser and New Beetle.

Today's fleet is both more comfortable and safer than the generation of '70s-era Pontiac GTOs. Higher-tensile steels enable manufacturers to make frames that vibrate less and are stiffer and lighter than old models. "Airflow management" is now a priority—with windshields shaped to reduce wind so you can actu-

PT CRUISER

LEXUS SC-430

CHEVROLET SSR

AUDI A4 CABRIOLET

about the sexy beasts: they can be profit machines, and they drive showroom traffic, bathing an otherwise humdrum line of sedans with an aura of cool. Honda's S2000, for example, is a curvaceous hot rod that's a hit with critics and customers. Honda limits supply to maintain overheated demand, so you can forget about a rebate. But volume isn't the point. Says spokesman Andy Boyd: "We want people to think Honda is about cars that are sporty and fun."

Automakers have also learned that a convertible need not handle like a Porsche to turn a profit. Consider Toyota's Solara convertible, based on an aging Camry platform. Toyota grafted a soft top onto the Solara with minimal changes elsewhere, and sold 7,600 ally hear more than the bass notes on that nine-speaker stereo.

Airflow management, however, may not be the ragtops' big draw. Consider the Massey family of Birmingham, Ala. Brothers Mark and James, both fathers in their 30s, say they're happy cruising in their mid-priced Mitsubishi Eclipse Spyders. "At almost every red light," says Mark, "someone wants to race me." That rebel spirit is catchy. After their mother June—a 60-year-old nurse—took a spin, she bought a Spyder too. ■

CADILLAC XLR: Like the Chevy and PT Cruiser models above, Caddy's convertible is not yet on sale

United We Stumble

Business slumps, and Bush fires his economic team

DICK CHENEY, A FRIEND FROM THEIR DAYS TOGETHER in the trenches of the Ford Administration, lured Paul O'Neill from the executive suite at Alcoa and persuaded him to become George W. Bush's Treasury Secretary. Federal Reserve Chairman Alan Greenspan loved the choice, the Vice President boasted in private in late 2000—and surely what made Greenspan happy would tickle the markets too. Except it didn't work out that way. A respected executive whose blunt talk the President at first found refreshing, O'Neill never emerged as a convincing advocate for the Administration's economic policy—in part because he never accepted its central belief that the cure for any ill involves more tax cuts. So it made a kind of Washington sense that Cheney was the one to telephone O'Neill on Dec. 5 with the news that the President had decided "to make a change."

Within hours, White House economic adviser Lawrence Lindsey got a call from chief of staff Andrew Card. He wanted to meet the next day. In a time-honored Washington version of hara-kiri, Lindsey offered his resignation before he was fired, extending the purge that began when Securities and Exchange Commission (SEC) chairman Harvey Pitt resigned on election night [see p. 100]. Though the abruptness of the moves was startling—not least to the two men ousted—it wasn't entirely surprising. Bush's economic team had long been viewed as the weak link in a popular Administration, and both O'Neill and Lindsey were prone to gaffes that embarrassed the boss. "They lack the ability to conceive, the ability to execute and the ability to sell economic policy," said an Administration official. And that pretty much sums up both their job descriptions.

Only 4 days after the firings, headlines reflected the struggles of the sagging U.S. economy: UNITED AIRLINES DECLARES BANKRUPTCY. The filing by the world's second largest carrier came the week after the Federal Govern-

ment refused the troubled company's request for $1.8 billion in aid. Although the employee-owned airline has valuable routes, it suffers from high labor costs and comfy contracts. Pilots at rival Southwest, a pioneer in low-fare air travel, routinely fly nearly 80 hours a month; United pilots fly just over 50 hours, even in a busy month.

The United bankruptcy put the final stamp on a bad year for the U.S. economy, and Bush quickly put a new team in place. The President named John Snow, the chairman of CSX, one of the nation's largest railroads, and a former chairman of the Business Roundtable, as his new Secretary of the Treasury. Stephen Friedman, a former co-chairman of investment banker Goldman Sachs, was picked for Lindsey's White House job. And Bush appointed William Donaldson, the widely respected former head of the New York Stock Exchange and a co-founder of the investment firm of Donaldson, Lufkin & Jenrette, to replace Pitt at the SEC. The new team's mission for the economy is not unlike United's with its sagging airline—to get the darn thing off the ground. ∎

WHY O'NEILL'S NUMBER WAS UP

⬆ **33%** UNEMPLOYMENT

⬆ **167%** FEDERAL DEFICIT

⬆ **4%** INFLATION (CONSUMER PRICE INDEX)

OUT: PAUL O'NEILL   **IN: JOHN SNOW**

Inflation was low—but that was the only good sign for the U.S. economy in 2002

⬇ **45%** GDP GROWTH RATE

⬇ **20%** THE DOW

⬇ **18%** MORTGAGE RATES

FAST FORWARD

What's new? Pants that never stain, a virtual keyboard and even a tomato-juice vaccine

DAVID BLUMENFELD FOR TIME

DENNIS GALANTE FOR TIME

No Wires, All Ears
Inventors: Various
Availability: Now, $99 to $250
Cell phones are now wireless—so why aren't the headsets that go with them? More and more of them are, thanks to the new Bluetooth technology that connects digital components over short distances. Bluetooth earpieces let you tuck away your cell phone and still walk while you talk.

Tomato Vaccine
Inventor: Charles Arntzen
Availability: In development
The tomatoes above carry genes for diseases like the hepatitis A virus (HAV). Their juice, it is hoped, may supplement costly laboratory-produced vaccines, and help reduce the use of needles. Biologist Arntzen hopes to test his tomato juice on animals within a year, then on humans.

Magic Fingers
Inventors: Canesta and VKB
Availability: 2003
In this "virtual" keyboard for portable devices, a laser beam projects the outline of a keyboard and a monitor tracks your hand movements.

Zoom!
Inventor: Grant Taylor
Availability: Now, from $1,200
The Wheelman is a simple idea: it's a miniature motorcycle you ride like a skateboard. 'Nuf said?

License to Spill
Inventor:
Nano-Tex, LLC
Availability:
Now, $35
Nanotechnology? This year it landed in our laps. These pants have undergone a chemical treatment that gives them nanowhiskers, millions of tiny fibers one hundred-thousandth of an inch long that help the pants repel spills.

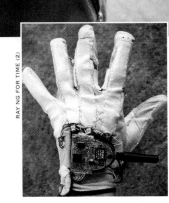

Hand to Mouth
Inventor: Ryan Patterson
Availability: Prototype
High school student Ryan Patterson, 18, created a device for the deaf that turns sign language into text. The glove senses its wearer's hand motions and transmits them wirelessly to a tiny handheld monitor, where they appear as words.

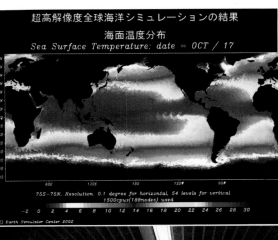

超高解像度全球海洋シミュレーションの結果
海面温度分布
Sea Surface Temperature: date = OCT / 17

75S-75N, Resolution 0.1 degree for horizontal, 54 levels for vertical
1500cpus(188nodes) used

(C) Earth Simulator Center 2002

Planet Tracker
Sorry, the Earth Simulator isn't for sale. Japan built the world's most powerful super-computer, below, to track global climate data, like ocean temperatures, left. Result: a virtual twin of our home planet.

Dust Bunnies, Surrender!
Inventor: iRobot
Availability: Now, $199
M.I.T. brainiacs created the battery-powered Roomba, a rechargeable robot vacuum that roams your house. Sensors help it avoid collisions.

Profile

Pitt Falls

When President Bush appointed Harvey Pitt, 57, chairman of the Securities and Exchange Commission, the business-friendly Republican in the Oval Office wanted a low-key ally of the financial industry to hold Wall Street's hand—a change of pace from Arthur Levitt, who had been a ferocious advocate for small

PITT **The SEC boss resigned under fire**

shareholders. Pitt, a respected attorney and former SEC employee, promised a "kinder and gentler" SEC—but that was before he was confronted with a cavalcade of business horror stories: Enron's collapse, the failure of Arthur Andersen and the flap over stock-analyst conflicts of interest.

In the fall Pitt blundered, naming former FBI Director William Webster, 78, to head up a new board that would monitor the accounting industry following the Enron/Arthur Andersen scandal. The SEC, bitterly divided along party lines, approved Webster, the G.O.P.'s choice for the slot, by a 3-to-2 vote. But Pitt didn't inform the commission that Webster sat on the board of U.S. Technologies, which had fired its outside auditor on his watch. The company was close to insolvent, its management under suspicion and its shareholders in court. Even G.O.P. Senator Richard Shelby joined Democrats in calling for Pitt's head. He resigned on the night of the November election.

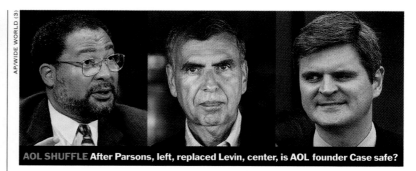

AOL SHUFFLE After Parsons, left, replaced Levin, center, is AOL founder Case safe?

AOL's Merger Mess

Less than three years after old-media giant Time Warner (parent company of TIME magazine) hitched its star to new-media giant America Online, investors weren't feeling so starry-eyed. By fall 2002, the third most widely held stock in the U.S. had lost some 65% of its value, as the once high-flying AOL stock came down to earth amid revelations of questionable accounting practices, inflated sales projections and dwindling revenues. By June, CEO Gerald Levin was out, replaced by former banker and famously steady hand Richard Parsons; AOL's chief booster, Bob Pittman, was canned, and Time Warner execs were promoted to run AOL. By fall, as the stock continued to struggle, rumors swelled that if board member Ted Turner had his way, board chairman and AOL founder Steve Case might be next to go.

Attack of the Bad Ad Boys

Marketers trying to reach trend-setting young urban males have discovered what Hollywood has long known: guys love troublemakers. Celebrity endorsers have typically been squeaky-clean family

Roundup

SMILE: Listerine PocketPaks are stamp-size, gel-coated pieces of paper that dissolve on the tongue and deliver a burst of mouthwash

SOLED! Sales of Dr. Scholl's sandals, a '70s fave, rose 630% after Sarah Jessica Parker wore them on HBO's *Sex in the City*

Hot Items

America—land of ingenuity. Companies made hay in 2002 by concocting nifty new products that satisfied cravings you might not even have known you had. From a high-tech mop to a handy new delivery system for fighting halitosis to a retread of a once-loved shoe line, here is a quick review of some of the hottest products of 2002.

WIRED—NOT! Samsung has the hot hand in gizmos—the Nexio is a pocket-size, color-monitor PC that gets to the Internet without wires

FLOORED: The Swiffer, a next-generation mop, employs disposable pads and has a container of cleaning fluid built into the handle

Image

Cargo Hold

Ships idle off the coast of California, left, unable to unload cargo, as a 10-day October lockout of union workers at 29 major Pacific ports seriously disrupted the nation's economy. Contract talks failed when unions charged modernization plans would eliminate jobs.

As millions of dollars of food spoiled on the docks and automakers chartered planes to fly parts to stalled assembly lines, President Bush became the first President in 25 years to invoke the Taft-Hartley Act to end a labor dispute.

men like Cal Ripken Jr. But today's ads often showcase figures known more for misdeeds than accomplishments. Among them: a Pony ad touting baseball's outcast gambler Pete Rose, below, for the Hall of Fame; basketball's alleged gun-wielding rampager, Allen Iverson, for Reebok; Hollywood's Academy Award–nominated actor Robert Downey Jr., who has been arrested for cocaine and heroin possession, for Skechers shoes.

WHY ISN'T PETE ROSE...

...IN THE HALL OF FAME?

PITCHER UP! Pete Rose, spokesman

HOUSING HOT SPOTS

Housing prices have been bubbly of late, but with interest rates low, economists say it's no bubble. Percentage change over the past year:

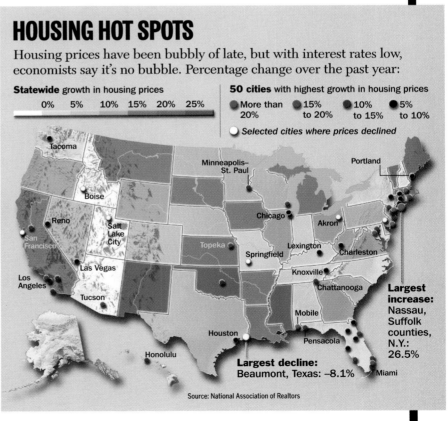

Statewide growth in housing prices
0% 5% 10% 15% 20% 25%

50 cities with highest growth in housing prices
● More than 20% ● 15% to 20% ● 10% to 15% ● 5% to 10%
○ *Selected cities where prices declined*

Tacoma · Minneapolis-St. Paul · Portland · Boise · Reno · Salt Lake City · Chicago · Akron · San Francisco · Topeka · Lexington · Charleston · Springfield · Las Vegas · Knoxville · Los Angeles · Tucson · Chattanooga · Mobile · Houston · Pensacola · Honolulu · Miami

Largest increase: Nassau, Suffolk counties, N.Y.: 26.5%

Largest decline: Beaumont, Texas: –8.1%

Source: National Association of Realtors

Photograph by Collen Trevor—Marathon Racing—Gamma

approves of sexual relations between adults and minors.

The most shocking aspect of the stories, however, was not the men's deeds but the church's response to them. Each of the accused priests had been transferred many times in the wake of repeated allegations of sexual abuse, but neither had ever been disciplined by his superiors until his case entered the civil court system.

As the extent of the allegations against the men grew, the spotlight turned on Bernard Cardinal Law, the Archbishop of Boston. The extraordinary tolerance Cardinal Law extended to both Geoghan and Shanley (and, if later accusations are correct, other U.S. bishops offered to similarly accused priests) indicated that the church's problems reached far deeper than rampant sexual misconduct. The crisis painted a picture of a complacent church leadership that was as out of touch with its flock as it was unable to control rogue priests—and far more concerned with squelching scandal than with protecting innocent young people.

In fact, the two revelations turned out to be the first drops in a deluge that nearly swamped the church. By June, more than 300 additional lawsuits had been filed against Catholic dioceses in 16 states, alleging thousands of instances of sexual abuse and subsequent cover-ups. More than 250 priests had been dismissed or forced to retire. In Maryland alone, one accused priest hanged himself in his room at a mental hospital, and another was shot three times (he survived) by a man who accused the cleric of molesting him nine years earlier, when the shooter was 17 years old. Adding to the flood of bad news were numerous reports of out-of-court payoffs by church officials to keep accusations of abuse secret.

As the sweep of the scandals sunk in, Catholic dioceses around the country faced the possibility of civil judgments that might collectively total more than $1 billion dollars. Francis Cardinal George of Chicago publicly speculated about having to sell the mansion in which that city's Cardinals have lived for more than a century in order to pay

abuse settlements. By mid-year, four bishops had stepped down over allegations that they had not acted decisively enough against sexual predators. The tremors led to a stern summons from Rome, where all of America's Cardinals gathered in April to hear Pope John Paul II deem the sexual abuse of children "not only a moral sin, but a crime."

THE BURGEONING CRISIS FINALLY GALVANIZED A PREviously somnolent church leadership. Assembling in Dallas two months after the Rome meeting, America's bishops broke with precedent: they devoted the entire conference to the subject of sexual abuse, and they allowed outsiders (translation: people other than bishops) to speak. A new tone was set by conference president Bishop Wilton Gregory in his opening remarks. "We are the ones," he declared, "whether through ignorance or lack of vigilance or, God forbid, with knowledge, who allowed priest abusers to remain in ministry and reassigned them to communities where they continued to abuse. Who worried more about the possibility of scandal than bringing about the kind of openness that helps prevent abuse."

Among the seven laypeople who addressed the conference were four survivors of abuse. A Catholic psychologist declared, "The protection of abusive priests is a sin, born of the arrogance of power." And a church historian concluded that "this scandal has brought home to laypeople how essentially powerless they are to affect its outcome and virtually anything else to do with the church."

The more than 250 bishops, representing 194 dioceses, seemed to get the message. They voted overwhelmingly to adopt a resolution that would remove from public ministry any priest found to have committed sexual offenses against a child (although the guilty party would still technically remain a priest). They agreed that each bishop must report abuse allegations involving minors to civil authorities, and they forbade dioceses to enter into confidentiality agreements in abuse settlements in most cases.

The conferees also created an independent commission, the Office for Child and Youth Protection, to monitor the church's performance on these issues. Oklahoma's Republican Governor, Frank Keating, a no-nonsense, law and order Catholic, agreed to lead it. The conference also agreed to submit the new charter to Rome for approval by the Pope.

The Vatican took its time in responding. After the April conclave, the Pontiff, now 82 and ailing, remained silent on the subject. In his place, Vatican officials weighed in at various times after the Dallas conference with unofficial suggestions that abusive

JIM BOURG—REUTERS—CORBIS

THE FLOCK: Suzy Nauman, right, leads the way as laypeople call the clergy to account outside the Cathedral of the Holy Cross in Boston on Mother's Day

priests not be referred to civil authorities for prosecution; that their records be kept secret; and that a policy of "zero tolerance" both exceeded the authority of American bishops and violated canon law. Some even suggested that the U.S. news media were largely to blame for the crisis.

Finally, in October, an order from the Vatican Congregation for Bishops, which speaks for the Pope in this area, called for the American bishops to revise the policy laid out in June, saying it did not sufficiently protect the rights of accused priests. A new commission was impaneled, comprised of four American bishops and four Vatican officials, to develop a new policy. For the U.S. bishops, the Vatican's rebuff crushed hopes that the crisis might be resolved quickly, rather than being allowed to fester and swell.

As plans for reform inched through the church's lab-

tice that they will no longer be covered for damages arising from sexual misconduct by priests if it can be shown that bishops knew or should have known about a pattern of similar behavior on the part of the offending priest.

O N NOV. 3, CARDINAL LAW STOOD IN THE PULPIT OF Boston's Cathedral of the Holy Cross and finally made the public confession his critics had long sought. "I acknowledge my own responsibility for decisions which led to intense suffering," he admitted, saying that he never meant to assign priests to positions where they could endanger children, but "the fact of the matter remains that I did assign priests who had committed sexual abuse."

Two weeks later, the U.S. bishops again convened, in Washington, D.C. Now they seemed to retrench: no out-

GEOGHAN: The plague of scandals that afflicted the church was set in motion when the Boston *Globe* broke the story of his long career as an alleged sexual abuser—30 years—during which time his superiors failed to remove him from pastoral duties

LAW: Heavily criticized for adopting a defensive posture early in the crisis, Boston's Cardinal found his authority undermined as events unfolded. After 58 diocesan priests signed a petition asking him to resign, he did so on Dec. 13

GREGORY: In contrast to Cardinal Law, the head of the U.S. bishops led the early calls for reform but seemed to backpedal at the bishops' fall meeting

yrinthine bureaucracies, the scandal was sparking immediate change among disillusioned American Catholics. Voice of the Faithful, a grass-roots organization of laypersons, began as an impromptu meeting of fewer than a dozen people after Mass one January Sunday in Wellesley, Mass.; by November, its membership rolls had grown to more than 10,000. The group is launching an ambitious campaign to reform the church from the bottom up and turn it into a representative democracy. Five bishops barred the group from using church facilities to meet within their dioceses. A separate group, the Survivors Network of those Abused by Priests, initiated a class action to void the confidentiality agreements that have been incorporated into many legal settlements with survivors of priestly abuse and have required those victims to remain silent.

Even the church's strongest supporters are troubled. Several groups of large donors to the church have begun to inquire about how their funds are spent and have found that, even in the best of times, diocesan financial affairs are a bit mysterious. And several large insurance carriers that cover dioceses against civil claims put their clients on no-

side speakers were allowed, and the Vatican's new policy was approved without amendment. It calls for all cases of sexual abuse by priests to be referred to the Vatican and for cases of priests who fight removal for such practices to be tried in front of closed church tribunals. And Bishop Gregory warned against "extremes within the church who have chosen to exploit the vulnerability of bishops in this moment"—words that further angered victims' groups.

John Geoghan (now a defrocked priest) has gone to jail. Convicted on a single count of molesting a 10-year-old boy in 1991 and serving a sentence of up to 10 years, he is awaiting trial on numerous other charges. Paul Shanley, on the other hand, is still a priest and claims to have done nothing wrong. He was indicted in June on 10 counts of child rape and six counts of indecent assault and battery. But one man's fate is settled. With the crisis still inflaming his flock, Cardinal Law flew to Rome and met with the Pope, who accepted his resignation on Dec. 13. Said Law: "It is my fervent prayer that this action may help the Archdiocese of Boston to experience the healing, reconciliation and the unity which are so desperately needed." Amen. ■

Now Playing: Women on a Binge

Have one more! Out-of-control drinking is the rage among young women

PHOTOGRAPH FOR TIME BY SHANNON STAPLETON—GAMMA

WASTED: A student partying in Florida on spring break keeps pace with the guys by attempting to chug a "beer bong"

AT THE UNIVERSITY OF COLORADO AT BOULDER, WOMEN like to brag that they can match men in alcohol consumption. Sarah, 21, describes a "kegstand"—two friends suspend you by your ankles over a keg, and you guzzle as much cheap beer as quickly as you can—and beams: "There are girls who can go longer than guys!" It's not just other girls who are keeping track either. "Here, if a girl gets drunk, it's, 'You're awesome,'" says Don Groves, who graduated from the university in December. School officials are not awed: frequent binge drinking among campus women rose 67% between 1993 and 2000.

Throughout the 1990s, it was mainly frat boys who generated headlines for waking up hazed and dazed in the ER—if they woke up at all. In recent years, however, some colleges have found a new cause for concern: young women who drink as dangerously as, if not more so than, their male classmates. Since 1999, some 16,000 men but more than 19,000 women have requested screening for alcohol abuse at federally funded day-long clinics held each spring at about 400 colleges.

Individual schools have found their own gauges for the trend. Counselors at Stanford University have observed an uptick in women who "regretted having sex" while drunk. Georgetown University has seen a 35% rise in women

sanctioned for alcohol violations over the past three years.

Simple observation tells us that women tend to get drunk more quickly than men. Now we're learning precisely why: women's bodies have a higher ratio of fat to water, so alcohol is less diluted when it enters the bloodstream. They also have lower levels of an enzyme that helps break down alcohol. But to public health officials, the most worrisome outgrowth of young women's shifting drinking patterns is a perceived shift in their sexual activities. A study of high school alcohol-dependent students published in March by the Pittsburgh Adolescent Alcohol Research Center found that 1 in 5 girls was infected with the herpes virus. Drunken women also suffer disproportionately from rape and sexual assault.

The trend isn't limited to alcohol. Young men are still more likely than young women to get arrested, crash their cars or fight in school. But while men's rates of risky behavior are falling, women's are either holding steady or rising. After falling from 40% in 1977 to 26% in 1992, the proportion of high school senior girls who smoke cigarettes rocketed back up to 35% in five years. And since 1991 the number of women arrested for aggravated assault has increased a staggering 46%, while the number of men arrested decreased 9.5%. You've come a long way, baby. ■

TRENDS OF THE YEAR

Yurts, Klimt & Toile? No, it's not a law firm—it's the new look of America in 2002

Trampolines

Boing! The highest-flying fad of 2002 was the humble tramp. Eminem bounced on one in his concerts, and TNN debuted a basketball-on-tramps game, "slamball." Snowboarders say bouncing refines their moves; fitness buffs say it keeps them limber. Pediatricians say, Be careful!

COURTESY TREEHOUSE WORKSHOP

TOM BEAN—CORBIS

Yurts and Treehouses

Part tent, part hut, a yurt is a small, round, roofed structure long used by Asian nomads. Easy to build and cheap to heat, new prefab yurts are the hottest news in shelter—next to a spreading interest in luxury treehouses.

Jeans

Once upon a time, denims came in two or three styles and a couple of colors. Now the selection is staggering: low rise, stone-washed, sanded, distressed, boiled, whiskered, shredded. The year's hippest brands: Diesel, Seven and Earl.

Toile

It's everywhere, so you'd better learn how to pronounce it (just say *twall*). The 18th century French fabric that shows countryside scenes was once found only on furniture—now it's at home on dog beds, handbags, PJs and golf bags.

Massage

Once a treasured perk of movie stars and the wealthy, massage is now enjoyed by more and more Americans. The portable massage chair, invented in 1987, has made the rubdown the fast food of health care. Today you can get rubbed the right way just about anywhere—even your local grocery store.

Klimt

It's not even a big anniversary: Viennese artist Gustav Klimt was born 140 years ago. But now his gold-tinged, sensual works—once scorned—are popping up in ads, restaurants and even on shoes. One sign he's this year's model: Cher copped his look for her concert posters.

Profile

A Master Departs

When couturier Christian Dior died suddenly of a heart attack in 1957, a jittery, bespectacled Algerian-born 21-year-old had to put the Dior show together. He came up with the trapeze, a dress that seemed to float away from the body as if by magic—or magnetism. The new look was a sensation. The

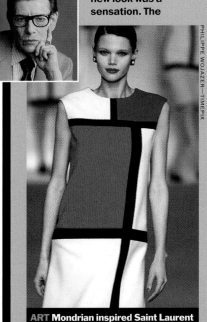

ART Mondrian inspired Saint Laurent

fashion press proclaimed, "Yves Saint Laurent has saved France!" A new design legend had arrived.

Saint Laurent left in January, retiring after a 46-year career in which he made trousers and suits chic for women and glamorized the pea coat, the leather biker jacket, the safari jacket and the peasant dress. He also found inspiration in the work of fine artists, turning the geometric paintings of Mondrian into chic, stop-traffic dresses. His brilliant use of color was as improbable as it was unerring.

Saint Laurent, 65, bowed out expressing scorn for the fashion industry's current reverence for marketing over craftsmanship. "Fashion ... has been reduced to mere window dressing," he told Paris Match. "Elegance and beauty have been banished."

BEFORE A tatty, comfy, suburban room | AFTER An uncomfy robo-metallic room

Rad Redos for Bad Pads

Think of it as the *Survivor* of home décor. The Learning Channel's home-makeover show *Trading Spaces*, on which pairs of neighbors assisted by an often domineering decorator, get two days and $1,000 to redo a room in each other's houses was the cable channel's most popular series in 2002. An adaptation of the British series *Changing Rooms*, the show is the ultimate rummage through your neighbors' medicine cabinet, or at least their overcluttered den. A traditional how-to show says your home expresses your personality. *Trading Spaces* says your home expresses your personality—and not everybody likes you. Each show

ends in a double climax, the "reveal." In this excruciating moment, host Paige Davis unveils the two remade rooms—and the pairs of neighbors do their best to smile through an aesthetic head-on collision.

Rosie, We Hardly Knew Ye

Well, it seemed like a good idea: both Martha Stewart and Oprah Winfrey had shown there was a huge market for magazines whose pages featured their ideas, whims, likes and dislikes. So, in April 2001, giant publisher Gruner + Jahr gave its 125-year-old women's magazine, *McCall's*, a makeover and put it into the hands of popular TV-talker Rosie O'Donnell. *Voilà—Rosie!* But in 2002 O'Donnell quit

Roundup

The Bench Weighs In

At the end of its 2001-02 term, the Supreme Court issued two major decisions. The Justices ruled 5 to 4 that public vouchers to pay for private schooling were legal. They also voted to restrict states from executing the mentally retarded in a 6-to-3 decision.

VOUCHERS: The court ruled on a challenge to Cleveland's program; 96% of its grants go to religious-school students

DEATH ROW: Twenty states currently permit the execution of the mentally retarded

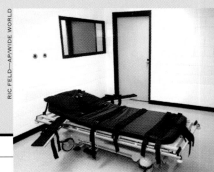

Graphic

Speak, Memory

In May linguists at Britain's University of Manchester surveyed the world's endangered languages, some of which have as few as three speakers. Here is a stat that will leave you speechless: experts say 50% of the world's 6,000 languages may be extinct by 2050, including Tofa, spoken by some 200 in Siberia, and Votic, used by 30 people in north Russia. Most Native American tongues are also on the endangered list.

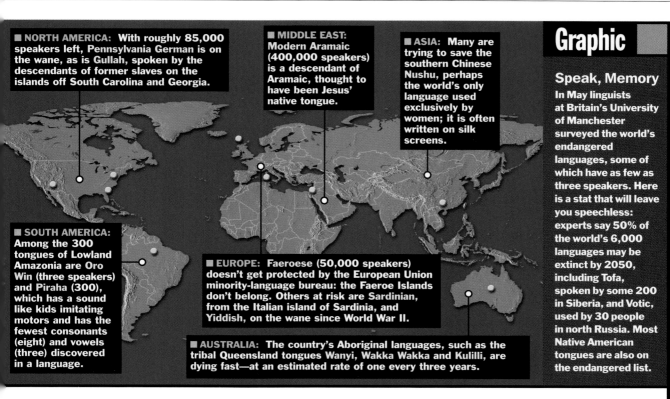

NORTH AMERICA: With roughly 85,000 speakers left, Pennsylvania German is on the wane, as is Gullah, spoken by the descendants of former slaves on the islands off South Carolina and Georgia.

MIDDLE EAST: Modern Aramaic (400,000 speakers) is a descendant of Aramaic, thought to have been Jesus' native tongue.

ASIA: Many are trying to save the southern Chinese Nushu, perhaps the world's only language used exclusively by women; it is often written on silk screens.

SOUTH AMERICA: Among the 300 tongues of Lowland Amazonia are Oro Win (three speakers) and Piraha (300), which has a sound like kids imitating motors and has the fewest consonants (eight) and vowels (three) discovered in a language.

EUROPE: Faeroese (50,000 speakers) doesn't get protected by the European Union minority-language bureau: the Faeroe Islands don't belong. Others at risk are Sardinian, from the Italian island of Sardinia, and Yiddish, on the wane since World War II.

AUSTRALIA: The country's Aboriginal languages, such as the tribal Queensland tongues Wanyi, Wakka Wakka and Kulilli, are dying fast—at an estimated rate of one every three years.

her TV show, shed her suburban-friendly persona, revealed she is a lesbian, got a new 'do … in short—to Gruner + Jahr's way of thinking—she took leave of her senses. After months of feuding, Rosie took leave of *Rosie*, saying she had been denied editorial control. Next, Gruner took leave of *Rosie*, folding it. The newsstand's loss is Court TV's gain: lawsuits are coming.

Where the Boys Are

Prepare to take sides: a battle of the sexes is brewing. The site is the Augusta National Golf Club in Georgia, home of the Masters Tournament. The élite club is rich in azaleas and strong in traditions: no blacks were invited to join its ranks until 1990, and women have never been allowed as members. After the 2002 Masters, Martha Burk, head of the National Council of Women's Organizations, asked Augusta chairman William (Hootie) Johnson to admit women. Johnson refused, declaring the club would remain open only to men, and saying that the 2003 Masters would be televised by CBS with no commercials, sparing tournament sponsors any fallout from his decision. Burk and her supporters vowed to press their cause.

Hunting Homebodies

As dwindling ranges and herds make hunting an increasingly difficult proposition for Americans,

JOHNSON: A showdown is brewing

EASY PICKINGS A hunter targets a ram

many hunters are shifting their shooting grounds from the wild to one of the country's rapidly growing number of hunting preserves. Up to 2,000 may exist in the U.S., with 500 in Texas alone. Most offer the ultimate prize: a guaranteed trophy.

Critics charge that the animals in these "canned hunts" are so tame as to make stalking them a travesty—and they point out that many of the animals slain are exotics: the Arabian oryx, the Nubian ibex, yaks, impalas and even the odd rhino, zebra or tiger. A few states ban or restrict the practice, and a pair of bills pending in Congress would prohibit the interstate sale of exotic animals for hunts. Supporters argue that exotics are bred in sufficient numbers to maintain their breeds.

Double, Double, Toil And Trouble: Scotland Rains on Tiger's Parade

Tiger Woods roared off to an incredible start in 2002, handily winning both the Masters Tournament and the U.S. Open. The long-hitting pro, now only 26, seemed on track to win all four of golf's most prestigious events in a single year—a feat he had already accomplished over the two seasons of 2000-01. Tiger was near the top after the first two rounds of the British Open at the Muirfield course in Scotland, but on the third day, nasty weather rolled in just as he teed off. When the misery was over, Tiger carded a 10-over-par 81, his worst round ever. The winner in a playoff: fan favorite Ernie Els, taking his third major title.

SLIP-SLIDIN' AWAY
His helmet proclaiming his patriotism, American
Jim Shea rips through a run in the skeleton event, a
one-man bobsled race. Inside the helmet is a picture of
Shea's grandfather, an Olympic champ in 1932.

EYES ON THE PRIZE

Focusing on fun, the Winter Games triumph over fears of terrorism—and a scandal or two

AS AMERICA PREPARED TO HOLD THE Winter Olympics for the first time since the Lake Placid Games of 1980, a pair of shadows loomed over the event. First, there was the humiliating fact that officials of the Salt Lake City Organizing Committee had been charged with bribing members of the International Olympic Committee to bring the Games to Utah. It was an embarrassment for America and especially for squeaky-clean Salt Lake City, home to the conservative Church of Jesus Christ of the Latter-Day Saints.

The second shadow was even darker: the Games were scheduled to begin only five months after the deadly attacks of 9/11/01. With America engaged in a war on terror, the security precautions in Utah were ratcheted up to unprecedented heights. More than 16,000 security personnel were in place to carry out the $310 million security plan—and that put the jitters into fans.

The fears of terrorism were largely dispelled by the moving opening ceremony. After a skirmish between U.S. and Olympic officials, the international body allowed a flag that had survived the attack on the World Trade Center to be included in the event. In the stands, 55,000 spectators stood in absolute silence as the tattered banner was borne into the arena by U.S. athletes and New York City fire fighters and police. Later, President George Bush shunned the dignitaries' heated luxury box to sit with the U.S. team, a simple gesture that significantly put the athletes—not security measures—first.

By the end of the Games, the shadows were forgotten. Over the next two weeks, America and the world watched entranced as the Winter Olympics were kick-started into the future: snowboarders brought a welcome youthful edge to the staid old events; an American became the first black athlete to win gold in the Winter Games; figure skating found a new star in Sarah Hughes, a chipper, charming 16-year-old.

There was one serious downer: a scandalous judging fix in the pairs skating event. Though it was rectified within days, the flap left many asking whether such show-biz events truly belonged under the Olympic umbrella.

So, sit back. It's 16° in the stands and a light snow is falling, but that's O.K.— George Bush is adding a few important words to the traditional opening statement: "On behalf of a proud, determined and grateful nation, I declare open the Games of Salt Lake City …" ■

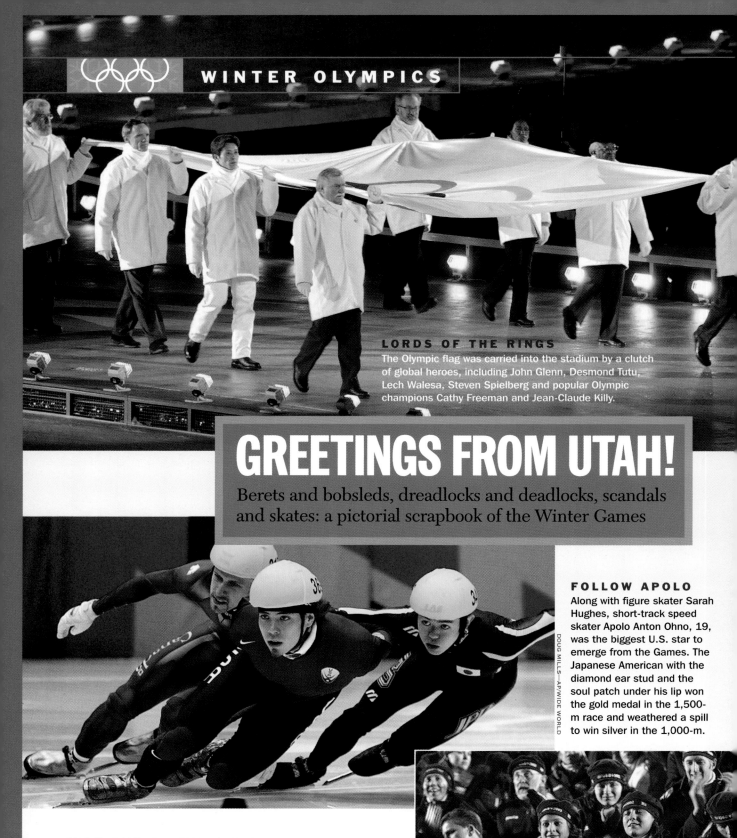

LORDS OF THE RINGS
The Olympic flag was carried into the stadium by a clutch of global heroes, including John Glenn, Desmond Tutu, Lech Walesa, Steven Spielberg and popular Olympic champions Cathy Freeman and Jean-Claude Killy.

GREETINGS FROM UTAH!

Berets and bobsleds, dreadlocks and deadlocks, scandals and skates: a pictorial scrapbook of the Winter Games

FOLLOW APOLO
Along with figure skater Sarah Hughes, short-track speed skater Apolo Anton Ohno, 19, was the biggest U.S. star to emerge from the Games. The Japanese American with the diamond ear stud and the soul patch under his lip won the gold medal in the 1,500-m race and weathered a spill to win silver in the 1,000-m.

DOUG MILLS—AP/WIDE WORLD

JUST ONE OF THE GANG
No, he didn't lose his beret. In a gesture that seemed just right— and helped defuse the concerns over terrorism that preceded the Games—George Bush sat with the U.S. athletes during the opening ceremony. When Sasha Cohen handed Bush her cell phone, the figure skater's surprised Mom got some ear-time with the Prez.

FASHION STATEMENT

Trés chic! When the American Olympians marched into the stadium during the opening ceremonies, they sported nifty blue-and-red berets. Before you could say Jacques Robinson, the style went to Americans' heads: the berets became the must-have gear of the Games. Below, Sherri Steele and daughters Madeline and Sydney feel the magic.

REUTERS—CORBIS

AMY SANCETTA—AP/WIDE WORLD

OFF WITH A BANG

Bizarre amalgams of pure cornpone, high-tech spectacle, local boosterism and p.c. cant, the ceremonies that open the Olympics occupy a campy niche in the world of extravaganza that is rivaled only by Super Bowl half-time shows. Salt Lake City's opener proffered cowboys and Indians, Mormon pioneers and a tad called "the Child of Light" (don't ask).

WHO OWNS THE ICE?

Admit it: the world is badly out of joint when the Canadians aren't the Olympic champions in hockey. In Utah they took both the men's and women's gold; above, the men's team celebrates after beating Finland 2-1 in the quarterfinals. The secret: the Canadian firm that installed the ice rink buried a Canadian dollar, or "loonie," beneath its surface.

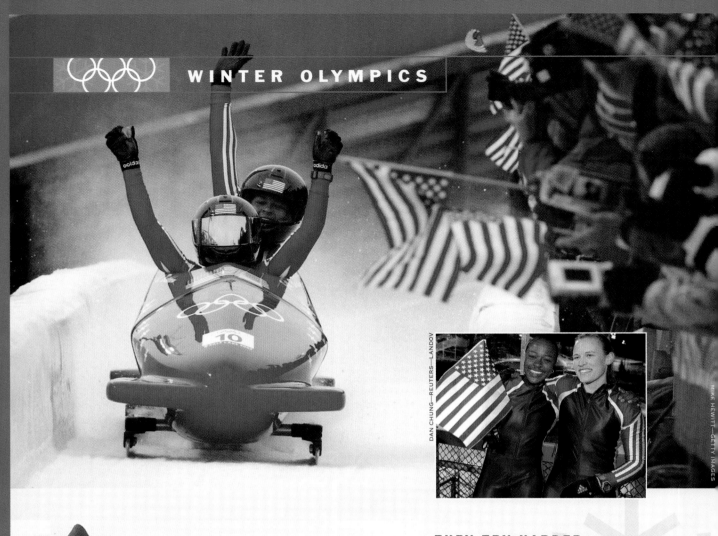

DAN CHUNG—REUTERS—LANDOV

MIKE HEWITT—GETTY IMAGES

JEFF J MITCHELL—REUTERS—LANDOV

THEY TRY HARDER

Vonetta Flowers and Jill Bakken weren't even the No. 1 U.S. female bobsled team; that honor belonged to Jean Racine and Gea Johnson. But when the runs were over, Bakken, 25, and Flowers, 28, placed first—a special joy for Flowers, a former college track star who became the first black athlete in history to win an Olympic event.

GOLD, GLORY AND GRIEF

Jim Shea exults with his father Jim Sr. after taking gold in the men's skeleton event. The Sheas are America's only three-generation Olympians. Jim Sr. competed in cross-country skiing in 1964. His father, Jack Shea, won two speed-skating medals in 1932. Sadly, Jack died at 91 in a car crash just weeks before the Utah Games began.

CHARLIE BOOKEER—AP/WIDE WORLD

THE CLARK ASCENDING

Kelly Clark, 18, is on her way to bringing home the first gold medal for the U.S. in the Games with a spirited run through the snowboarding halfpipe course. Judges call it amplitude; fans call it "big air." Whatever: Clark simply soars higher than anyone else.

GOLDEN GIRL

A born crowd pleaser, Tristan Gale, 21, gets slap-happy after her first run in the skeleton event. Before the final run, she streaked her dreadlocks red, white and blue—then she streaked down the hill to beat teammate Lee Ann Parsley by one-tenth of a second and take the gold.

BODE-ACIOUS

Bode Miller, 24, came from behind twice to win silver, first in the Alpine combined event, then in the grand slalom. But his bid to become the first American to win three Alpine skiing medals in one Games came up short when he finished 25th in the final slalom event.

DAVID J. PHILLIP—AP/WIDE WORLD

SKATING'S NEW STAR

Leaping, spinning, flowing—and charming—her way to first place in figure skating, American Sarah Hughes vaulted over such favorites as America's Michelle Kwan and Sasha Cohen and Russia's Irina Slutskaya. Hughes, only 16, took time off from her junior year in high school in Great Neck, N.Y., to compete. In fourth place after the short program, she landed an unprecedented pair of triple-triple jumps in her long routine, then fell to the floor backstage when she learned she had won. It was a tough night for six-time U.S. champion Kwan, below, who stumbled in her routine but was gracious in her disappointment.

A JUDGING SCANDAL TARNISHES SKATING

As they laced up for the figure-skating pairs final in Salt Lake City, Canadians Jamie Salé and David Pelletier were not without their critics. Their routine was two years old. Their music was the theme from *Love Story,* which came off as a bit sappy compared with the more nuanced choice—Jules Massenet's *Thaïs*—of Russians Yelena Berezhnaya and Anton Sikharulidze. Looking over the roster of judges, many people expected a kind of cold war face-off. The judges from the U.S., Canada, Germany and Japan were more likely to back the Canadians.

Center. The door was sealed with thick tape that kept prying reporters from eavesdropping. It also prevented them from hearing the weeping of Le Gougne, who sobbed to the astonished judges that her decision had been coerced. Le Gougne claimed she had voted for the Russian skaters at the direction of the French skating federation and its president, Didier Gailhaguet.

Gailhaguet denied the claims and suggested that pressure was brought upon Le Gougne from "left and right"—implying that it came from Canadian skating officials as well. Happily, justice

EFORE **The shocked Canadians eyeball the winning Russian team**

AFTER **Justice is done. Salé, Pelletier and the Russians are all smiles**

The Russians could probably count on the judges from China, Russia, Ukraine and Poland. That would leave the French judge, Marie-Reine Le Gougne, as the deciding vote.

But the Russians did not skate their best. Berezhnaya and Sikharulidze had as many as six flaws in their program, notably Sikharulidze's stumble on the side-by-side double Axel. Berezhnaya's landings on the throw jumps were also not as smooth as Salé's. In contrast, Salé and Pelletier were a miracle of unity.

Then came the astonishing vote. The technical scores for the Canadians were all high, but the scores for presentation favored the Russians, 5-2 (with two tie votes), with the French vote in their camp. Salé and Pelletier looked briefly stunned. The crowd of some 16,000 at the Salt Lake Ice Center exploded in boos. The possibility of a judge's deal was in the air immediately. The Russians were eager to sustain a long tradition of winning the gold medal for pairs skating—10 Olympic Games in a row. The French wanted just as badly to win gold in the ice dance event, where Russian-born Marina Anissina and Gwendal Peizerat were France's only real shot at a first place in skating.

Early the next morning, the nine judges of the pairs event and two referees convened in a windowless basement room of the Ice

was rendered by Jacques Rogge, the new president of the International Olympic Committee. Within the week, a beaming, exultant Salé and Pelletier were awarded gold medals of their own— a popular and unusually expedient move by the IOC.

All's well that ends well? No. The scandal resurfaced in August, when Italian and U.S. officials fingered Alimzhan Tokhtakhounov, 53, a bull-headed Uzbek long linked with the Russian Mafia, as the mastermind of the fix. Also implicated were the French ice-dance team of Anissina and Peizerat. Anissina and her mother were caught on tape talking with Tokhtakhounov. In one call, the Uzbek promised, "We are going to make your daughter an Olympic champion. Even if she falls, we will make sure she is No. 1." A U.S. grand jury was investigating the charges in the fall.

Whatever the truth turns out to be, international figure skating and the Olympic movement itself have been shaken. A chorus of voices is asking whether figure skating even belongs in the Games. But the skaters may not depart anytime soon. The smiley dudes on their snowboards may be the wave of the future. For now, though, when it comes to making the Winter Games a global fascination and a very considerable cash machine, it's the Brian Boitanos and Michelle Kwans of the world who count most. ∎

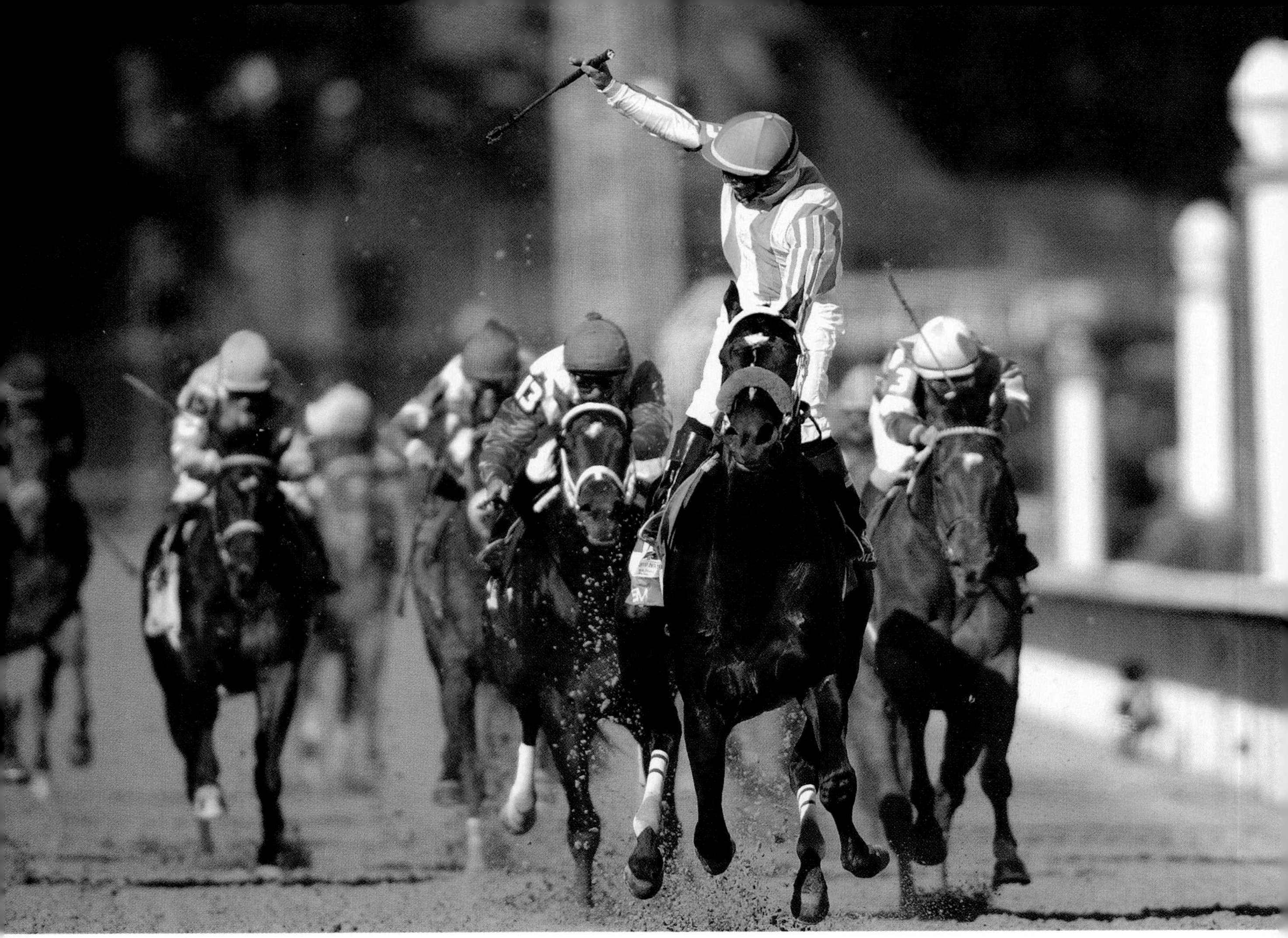

GAMERS

A high-five, suck-it-up, dig-deep photo gallery of the rare athletes who do their best under pressure

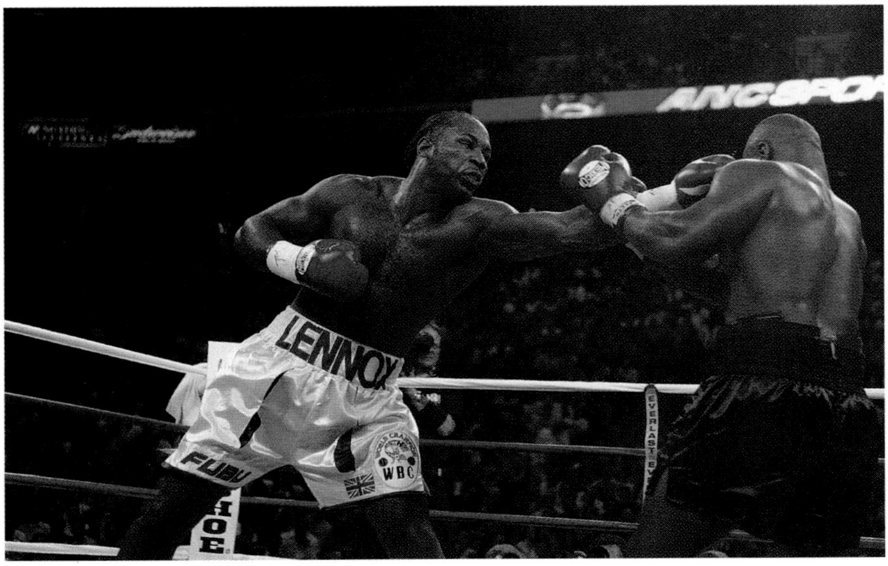

AL BELLO—GETTY IMAGES

War Emblem
Racing's new black beauty made a strong run at the Triple Crown, taking the Kentucky Derby as a 20-to-1 shot—leading from gate to wire—then easily winning the Preakness. But the ornery colt, a natural front runner, stumbled coming out of the gate at the Belmont Stakes and finished eighth.

Lennox Lewis
The 6-ft. 5-in. British heavyweight beat Mike Tyson twice—first in a prefight scuffle at a press conference (where Iron Mike bit Lewis' leg), then in their June 8 title match in Memphis. Lewis simply outboxed Tyson, landing hundreds of methodical punches over eight rounds that left Mike whipped.

Paula Radcliffe

What a run! The British whiz, 28, won major races at 3,000- 5,000- and 10,000-m lengths in the summer, then outran the field to set a new world record for women (2:17:18) at the Chicago Marathon in October.

Lisa Leslie

The gifted center reigned over the WNBA once again, leading her L.A. Sparks to a second league title (she was the tourney MVP) and becoming the first woman pro to dunk the ball.

Barry Bonds

Some season: a .370 batting average, 46 home runs, 110 RBI's, an amazing on-base percentage of .582 —and a record fifth MVP award. But no Series ring!

Ernie Els

South Africa's "Big Easy," 32, was golf's Next Big Thing—B.T. (Before Tiger). The two-time U.S. Open champ, slumping in recent years, regained his form and won the British Open in a four-way playoff.

ON TOP OF THE WORLD

Billions agree: soccer's World Cup is the greatest show on earth

WORLD UNITED? IN THE GRIM YEAR 2002, THAT DREAM seemed very far away—except during a few weeks in June, as eyes from Pakistan to Portugal to Paraguay turned to Asia, where Japan and South Korea played host to soccer's quadrennial extravaganza, the World Cup. Files from TIME's international correspondents reported scenes that were strikingly similar in cultures that are otherwise strikingly different.

Beijing. A thousand fans gathered outside the Worker's Stadium, sucking on tallboys of Tsingtao and watching a big-screen broadcast of their country's maiden World Cup game. It was by far the most sensitive day on China's

political calendar—June 4, the 13th anniversary of the Tiananmen massacre—and here was an uncontrolled public event in a country where people are warned on National Day to stay home and watch fireworks on TV. China lost 2-0 to Costa Rica. The crowd departed quietly.

Kashmir. As shells rained down across the Line of Control, killing three outside the India-administered border town of Poonch, fans gathered around the few TV sets in the leafy summer Kashmiri capital of Srinagar to watch England vs. Argentina. "When daily one sees and hears about people getting killed, watching the World Cup may sound unthinkable," said civil engineer Farooq Ahmed

Khan. "But how else do we escape the mental agony?"

South Africa. In Johannesburg's Soweto, the sprawling black township that came to symbolize the oppressive apartheid regime, living standards have risen, and most homes now have TVs. But locals like to gather at Wandie's, a pub and restaurant with South African staples like pap (corn flour porridge) and mutton stew. "Stand up for the national anthem," ordered Wandie's owner, Wandie Ndala, before South Africa's match against Slovenia. Minutes later the crowed roared as South Africa grabbed the lead.

Fortunately, in this Cup the fans' intensity was matched by the quality of the play. In perhaps the most surprising series of contests in Cup history, longtime favorites fell to up-and-coming new teams. Reigning champion France was toppled by Senegal, a former colony. Italy and Argentina were ousted early. Host South Korea—not on anyone's list of soccer powers—harnessed the energy of a sea of red-clad fans and clawed their way to fourth place.

To the delight of America's long-suffering soccer fans,

SOLE POWER: Left, Germany's Dietmar Hamann goes one on one with Ronaldo of Brazil in the Cup final. Brazil won, 2-0. Center: U.S. captain Claudio Reyna celebrates with fans after America's 2-0 victory over Mexico in the second-round playoff match in South Korea. Inset, U.S. coach Bruce Arena exults after the Mexico game; he was widely credited with America's strong finish. Right, Brazil's captain, Cafu, elevates the Cup after the final.

who remain convinced their favorite sport will be the national pastime any day now, an accomplished and inspired U.S. team held its own in the tournament, upsetting both Portugal and Mexico to reach the quarterfinals—and avenging a humiliating last-place finish in 1998.

When the dust settled, though, it was Germany and Brazil, two of soccer's legendary teams, that faced off in the final. An inspired Brazilian squad seemed to find its magical touch again, and at the end of the match, a united world hailed one of the most memorable of all Cups. Well, an almost united world: there was no joy in Berlin. ■

Profile

No Longer a Kid

When point guard Jason Kidd took the long-hapless New Jersey Nets all the way to the brink of the 2002 NBA championship, his triumph was both professional and personal: in 2001 the four-time NBA All-Star had been arrested for allegedly punching his wife Joumana in the face. It was only the most recent in a chain of incidents that painted the ultra-

KIDD Going up for two—and growing up too

competitive Kidd as yet another of professional sport's growing roster of loutish thugs. Since joining the pro ranks in 1994—after only one year in college—Kidd has fathered a son out of wedlock, pleaded no contest to leaving the scene of an auto accident and been accused of hitting a woman at a party (no charges were filed).

In the 2001-02 season, Kidd, 29, joined the Nets—and finally grew up. Always a great passer, tough rebounder and stirring on-court leader, he became a fan favorite and led the Nets to the finals. "There's a calmness there," said Nets president Rod Thorn. "He has the ability to really heighten his focus under pressure." True—but in the finals, all Kidd's newfound maturity couldn't stop Shaquille O'Neal's unbeatable L.A. Lakers.

RALLY! The Angels' chimp is a champ

Angels Go Ape, Beat Bonds

The last time the San Francisco Giants played in a World Series, in 1989, the earth moved: game three was canceled after a major tremor hit the Bay Area. This time Giants fans were counting on their own natural phenomenon—slugger Barry Bonds—to win the Series for the first time since they were the New York Giants in 1954. Only one thing stood in their path: a toy chimp, dubbed the rally monkey, symbol of the once lowly Anaheim Angels, who were making their first Series appearance. In a terrific run of games, the final score was Angels & Monkey: 4; Bonds & Co.: 3.

The Man in the Arena

Bruce Arena has made a career of unexpected success. When he took over Major League Soccer's D.C. United in 1996 after an impressive college career, there were doubts he could handle pro players. United won back-to-back MLS Cup titles. When he was named coach of the U.S. men's team in October '98, there was clamoring that the team needed a leader with a glittering international résumé, not some guy from Brooklyn.

Now it has both. Rallying a U.S.

ARENA Comeback coach

team that had placed dead last in the 1998 World Cup, Arena took the team to wins over Portugal and Mexico, all the way to the Cup's quarterfinal round.

Roundup

TOUR DE FRANCE: Lance Armstrong went U.S. Postal for the fourth time, winning the great road race in a breeze

U.S. OPEN: In a match of two great veterans, Pete Sampras, 31, outlasted Andre Agassi, 32, in four sets to take the crown

The Usual Suspects

How to measure the difference between winning the Tour de France for the fourth year in a row—and the third? We can't tell you, and we're not sure Lance Armstrong could. So while we don't mean to slight the achievements of some of the world's best athletes, we decided to collect a few of the year's all-too-predictable champions in one place. Call it the downside of consistency.

REUTERS NEWSMEDIA—CORBIS

CHARADE? Harding and Jones act up

Let's Get Ready to Grumble

Discerning viewers know they can count on Fox TV to fill the yawning chasms in televised sports. Stymied because cockfighting and dwarf tossing are illegal, Fox devised another way to lure viewers: *Celebrity Boxing.* In the first of Fox's prime-time specials in this previously neglected realm, Long Island Lolita Amy Fisher was scheduled to duke it out with former Olympic skater Tonya Harding. When Fisher backed out, another tabloid heroine, presidential accuser Paula Jones, laced up. And the second bill: Partridge Family imp Danny Bonaduce vs. Barry Williams, a.k.a. Greg Brady. Who won? Who cares?

AFP—CORBIS

NBA CHAMPS: Kobe Bryant, left, and Shaquille O'Neal— once bitter enemies but now partners in domination—teamed up to bring the L.A. Lakers a third straight trophy. It's official: it's a dynasty

NABISCO CHAMP: Annika Sorenstam won the first women's golf major, finished second in the U.S. Open, second in the McDonald's LPGA— but missed the cut in the British Open

AP/WIDE WORLD

Image

Adieu, Slew
When Seattle Slew died at 28 on May 7, he was the last surviving winner of the Triple Crown, which he achieved, almost without serious competition, in 1977.
The stallion won 14 of 17 starts, made $1.2 million and went on to sire 102 stakes winners, including 1984 Kentucky Derby winner Swale and 1992 Horse of the Year A.P. Indy. Railbirds recall that when Slew went up against fellow Triple Crown winner Affirmed in the 1978 Marlboro Cup, Slew won by three lengths.

The Top Sorority in Tennis

This year tennis fans got the finals matches they had been looking forward to for years: sisters Venus and Serena Williams battled for three major championships.

While it would be nice to report that the sisters brought out the best in each other, engaged in tense rallies, divvied up the titles and are poised for many more years of glorious duels, the truth is much more stark: little sister Serena, 20, simply stomped Venus, 22. Worse, as fans noted, when the two face each other across the net, they never seem to bring their best game.

Serena's string started at the French Open, where 115 of the match's 149 points ended in unforced errors. The two played their most exciting match at Wimbledon, with Venus rallying to force a tiebreaker in the first set. But Serena won it and cruised to a 6-3 win in the second. At the U.S. Open, Serena was once again far more steady than Venus, who made 33 unforced errors, including 10 double faults. One solution: the return in 2003 of Lindsay Davenport and Martina Hingis, both injured in 2002, should expand the field of top players.

FRED MULLANE—NEWSPORT—CORBIS

SERENA Unbeatable in the majors

Refitted with New Eyes, The Hubble Telescope Records Fresh Wonders

On April 2, 2002, the Hubble telescope trained one of its powerful new eyes, the Advanced Camera for Surveys (ACS), on an object in the constellation Monoceros called the Cone Nebula. The new camera, installed by shuttle astronauts during an overhaul mission to the Hubble in March, took this beautiful image of a giant pillar of gas and dust that is a seedbed of star formation. This picture shows only one-third of the entire Cone Nebula, which is seven light-years long. The red halo of light surrounding the nebula is created when ultraviolet radiation heats the gas and sets the stardust glowing.

HALO OF STARS:
In this galaxy, known
as Hoag's Object,
younger bright-blue
stars form a ring
around a core of older
yellow stars. The
entire formation is
about 120,000 light-
years wide, slightly
larger than our Milky
Way Galaxy

STARDUST VISIONS

A gallery of mind-bending outer-space images, class of '02

L AUNCHED IN 1990, THE HUBBLE SPACE TELESCOPE
keeps getting better. In March 2002 shuttle astronauts installed a powerful new eye on it, the
Advanced Camera for Surveys (ACS). Two of the
deep-space pictures on this page were taken by the
ACS; two more are from other Hubble cameras. The
close-up of the sun's corona was taken by the TRACE
satellite, which NASA launched in 1998.

NASA is now looking beyond Hubble. In 2002 the
space agency awarded an $825 million contract to
TRW Inc. for the new James Webb Space Telescope.
Planned to launch in 2010, it will orbit 940,000 miles
above the earth, then unfold a segmented light-
gathering mirror 20 ft. in diameter—more than twice
as large as the Hubble's. The new scope will focus on
infrared views, but NASA says it will take visible-light
pictures as well—they know they've got us hooked. ■

HOT! This image of the sun's corona
was taken by the Transition Region and
Coronal Explorer Satellite (TRACE),
which studies the solar surface and winds

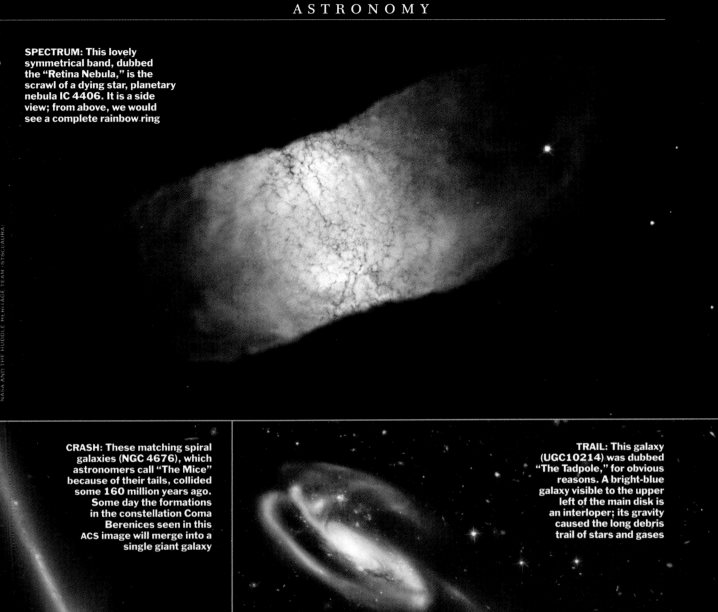

SPECTRUM: This lovely symmetrical band, dubbed the "Retina Nebula," is the scrawl of a dying star, planetary nebula IC 4406. It is a side view; from above, we would see a complete rainbow ring

NASA AND THE HUBBLE HERITAGE TEAM (STSCI/AURA)

CRASH: These matching spiral galaxies (NGC 4676), which astronomers call "The Mice" because of their tails, collided some 160 million years ago. Some day the formations in the constellation Coma Berenices seen in this ACS image will merge into a single giant galaxy

TRAIL: This galaxy (UGC10214) was dubbed "The Tadpole," for obvious reasons. A bright-blue galaxy visible to the upper left of the main disk is an interloper; its gravity caused the long debris trail of stars and gases

NASA, H. FORD (JHU), G. ILLINGWORTH (USCS/LO), M. CLAMPIN (STSCI), G. HARTIG (STSCI), THE ACS SCIENCE TEAM, AND ESA

LAST COMMON ANCESTOR
Both chimps and humans are believed to have descended from a single apelike primate that remains to be discovered

Latest find (Toumai)

Sahelanthropus tchadensis

Orrorin tugenensis

Ardipithecus ramidus kadabba

Ardipithecus ramidus ramidus

Australopithecus anamensis

Kenya...

A. bahrelg...

A. afare... (includes "L...

LIBYA

AFRICA

CHAD

NIGER

Site of latest discovery

Lake Chad

★ N'Djamena

SUDAN

Red Sea

SAUDI ARABIA

ERITREA

YEMEN

"Lucy" A. afarensis

Ardipithecus ramidus ramidus

Addis Ababa ☆

DJIBOUTI

SOMALIA

Ardipithecus ramidus kadabba

A F R I C A

OUT OF THE MAINSTREAM
Sahelanthropus tchadensis was discovered 1,550 miles (2,500 km) from the fossil-rich Rift Valley

Great Rift Valley

ETHIOPIA

A. anamensis

KENYA

Indian Ocean

Orrorin tugenensis

★ Nairobi

500 mi.
500 km

New Kid on The Block

WALK LIKE A MAN

An ancient skull found in Chad shakes up mankind's family tree

ALIVE, THE CREATURE MIGHT HAVE RESEMBLED AN ordinary chimpanzee to our eyes. In death, however, it sent shock waves through the world of science. After eight grueling years of hunting in central Africa, researchers uncovered one of the most sensational fossil finds in living memory: the well-preserved skull of a chimp-size animal, probably a male, that doesn't fit any known species. According to paleontologist Michel Brunet of the University of Poitiers in France, whose team reported the find in *Nature* in July, there is no way it could have been an ape of any kind. It was almost certainly a hominid,

a member of a subdivision of the primate family whose only living representative is modern man. And it left scientists gasping with astonishment for several reasons.

First, it is nearly 7 million years old—a million years more ancient than the previous record holder. More surprising, unlike all the record setters of the past three decades, the skull wasn't found near the Great Rift Valley of East Africa. Instead, it turned up in the sub-Saharan Sahel region of Chad, more than 1,500 miles to the west, forcing a rethinking of the current theories about where humans arose.

Most remarkable of all, though, is the skull itself. The

A. garhi

A. africanus

...ethiopicus

A. boisei

H. rudolfensis

Homo habilis

H. ergaster

H. erectus

A. robustus

H. antecessor

H. heidelbergensis

H. neanderthalensis

H. sapiens (modern humans)

Gorillas

Chimpanzees

...ILION

1 MILLION YEARS AGO

PRESENT

...just-announced
...elanthropus is so old
...most researchers believe it
...e very soon after the chimp-hominid
...t. But whether it was our direct ancestor or
...one of many hominid species that roamed the
...h at that time is a matter of vigorous debate

TIME Diagram by Ed Gabel; map by Lon Tweeten   Sources: *Nature*; American Museum of Natural History

creature, named *Sahelanthropus tchadensis* (roughly: "Sahel hominid from Chad"), has a mix of apelike and hominid features. Some paleontologists say the hominid features, especially the face, are a lot more modern-looking than might be expected at so early an evolutionary stage.

Paleontologists are scrambling to digest the implications of this remarkable find. It may simply be that the discovery fills in the evolutionary sequence—the so-called family tree—that leads to modern humans. But some argue that the new fossil could replace the idea of a tree with something more akin to a thick, bristly bush. This group says the emergence of humans may not have been a neat succession of increasingly modern-looking ancestors, but rather was an evolutionary brawl, with multiple species fighting for survival at just about every point in prehistory. Whatever the answer, says Daniel Lieberman, a biological anthropologist from Harvard, "this is one of the most important fossil discoveries in the past 100 years." ∎

HEAD MEN: Paleontologist Michel Brunet holds the skull of *Sahelanthropus tchadensis*, informally called Toumaï ("Hope of Life," in the local language). At left is college student Ahounta Djimdoumalbaye, who found the skull on July 19, 2001. News of the find was not made public until this year. Brunet's team—some 40 scientists from 10 countries—has found 10,000 fossils in Chad since 1994

PATRICK ROBERT—CORBIS SYGMA (2)

FULL FATHOM FINDS

Three marine missions illuminate the history of war at sea

A TRIO OF UNDERSEA OPERATIONS THAT SHED light on three historic wartime encounters made 2002 a memorable year for undersea exploration. Robert Ballard, perhaps the world's best-known underwater explorer, was involved in two of the searches. In 2000 Ballard's team probed the sea floor near Pearl Harbor in Hawaii, seeking a Japanese midget submarine believed to have been sunk on Dec. 7, 1941, but failed to find it. The sub was located by a Hawaii team in 2002, months after Ballard's team located the remains of John F. Kennedy's *PT-109* craft in the Solomon Islands. In August, the turret of the historic Civil War ironclad, the U.S.S. *Monitor*, was raised off the coast of Virginia. ■

WOUNDED: Union officers inspect the *Monitor*'s damaged turret after its battle with the *Virginia*

CORBIS

ON TARGET: The turret of the U.S.S. *Monitor* is visible through the bubble of the *Johnson-Sea-Link II* minisub

HELBER/EARLEY—POOL—AP/WIDE WORLD

HEART OF IRON

One hundred and forty years after its guns fell silent, the turret of the Union ironclad *Monitor* was pulled from the ocean in August. In a single battle on March 9, 1862, the *Monitor* and the Confederate ironclad *Virginia*—built on the raised hull of the sunken U.S.S. *Merrimack*—ended the era of wooden warships. The two ships pounded each other at close range but withdrew after neither of them could achieve an advantage. The *Monitor*, designed by John Ericsson, was distinguished by its rotating turret, which could fire on a target regardless of its position. At sea, only its turret and pilothouse were far above the surface; just 18 in. of the raft showed above the waterline.

The *Monitor* carried a crew of 19 men and officers; 16 died when it sank in a storm on Dec. 31, 1862. Human remains were found in the turret, which will be displayed at Newport News, Va., for at least the next decade. ■

SISTER SHIP: This HA-19 sub, a twin of the one found in 2002, was salvaged decades ago

U.S. NAVAL HISTORICAL CENTER PHOTOGRAPH

HUNTERS: Terry Kerby, left, and Rachel Shackelford helped find the midget sub

RONEN ZILBERMAN— AP/WIDE WORLD

A MINISUB FOUND

Resolving a mystery that had lingered since Dec. 7, 1941, a team from the Hawaii Undersea Research Laboratory located a Japanese minisub in August, just outside Pearl Harbor at a depth of 1,200 ft. The 78-ft.-long ship was one of five Japanese subs that had crept into Pearl Harbor in the hours before the surprise attack; all five were sunk by U.S. fire, historians believe. Three of the subs had already been accounted for; one is still missing.

Experts say this sub is the one sunk at 6:45 a.m. by the destroyer U.S.S. *Ward:* it has a bullet hole in the conning tower, and its torpedoes had not been fired. The missing sub had fired both its weapons. The find finally confirmed U.S. sailors' accounts of the historic day's first skirmish.

A HERO'S CRAFT

On May 29, shipwreck hunter Robert Ballard announced that his team had located the remains of the *PT-109*, the World War II patrol boat commanded by John F. Kennedy, in the Pacific Ocean off the Solomon Islands. The wooden boat sank in August 1943 after it was hit and cut in two by a Japanese destroyer. Its remains were lying 1,200 ft. below the surface in the Blackett Strait near Gizo in the New Georgia group of the Solomons.

After the crash, Kennedy and 10 other survivors swam 15 hours to reach a nearby island; the future President towed an injured crew member to safety by swimming with the man's life-jacket strap in his teeth. Ballard, who found the wreck of the *Titanic* in 1985, said the wreck will not be disturbed. ∎

YOUTH: U.S. Navy Lieut. John F. Kennedy aboard the *PT-109* in the Solomon Islands

COURTESY JFK LIBRARY, BOSTON

CLUE? This unfired torpedo is believed to be from the *PT-109*

NINE LIVES?

Here, kitty, kitty! Meet cc, the world's first cloned cat. Who's next?

WITH HER BIG ROUND EYES, HER BUTTON NOSE AND her I'm-ready-for-fun look, the kitten named cc (short for carbon copy or copy cat) has a face that's almost impossible not to love, which may help explain why the hostility that usually accompanies news on the cloning front was almost drowned out in February 2002 by the sound of the press corps cooing on cue.

Cc is the name the scientists behind the first cloned house pet gave their creation, a shorthaired calico that is a genetic (though not a visual) duplicate of her biological mom. Because she is so seductively cute—pulling at the same heartstrings an infant human clone would invariably

tug—she lays bare the emotional subtext that has so far been missing in the great cloning debate. It's one thing to argue the merits of cloning when you're talking about un-cuddly sheep, mice, cattle, goats and pigs. It's quite another when the clone is practically sitting in your lap, mewing and purring and begging for love.

And so a debate that began in 1997 with the cloning of Dolly the sheep took on a new urgency. Public opinion was once again split along ethical fault lines, although this time pro-cloners were joined by pet lovers and anti-cloners drew support from the A.S.P.C.A. and the Humane Society. "We must question the social purpose here," said Wayne

Pacelle, senior vice president of the Humane Society's U.S. branch. "Just because you're capable of something doesn't mean you should act on it."

Not that making cc was particularly easy. The work was overseen by Mark Westhusin, an associate professor at Texas A&M University's College of Veterinary Medicine, and backed by Genetic Savings & Clone, a private company whose financial benefactor wanted to clone not a cat but an aging border-collie mix named Missy. However, for reasons not fully understood, dogs' ova don't mature well in laboratory dishes. So after almost three fruitless years, Westhusin's team turned their attention from dogs to cats.

Working first with an adult male cat, they harvested cells from the animal's mouth and fused them with cat-donor eggs that had been emptied of genetic material. This created 82 embryos, which were implanted into seven surrogate mothers. The process yielded only a single fetal clone; it died in utero. Researchers then turned to cumulus cells from the ovaries of a female named Rainbow, creating five cloned embryos. These were implanted in Allie, another surrogate, and this time an embryo took hold and grew. The result was cc, born Dec. 22 and announced with a flourish in February by the journal *Nature*.

It was more than a mere scientific breakthrough. The news caught the eye of entrepreneurs. Each year millions of pets die in the U.S., leaving behind plenty of well-heeled owners who would be willing to pay top dollar to replicate their beloved companion. Genetic Savings & Clone already offers to freeze pet DNA for future cloning, charging a one-time fee of $895 plus $100 a year for storage.

But let the cloner beware. Genetically reproducing a pet is not cheap. There are also technical problems. The Texas lab's 1-in-87 success rate is typical of cloning work, which can produce dozens of dead embryos for every living one. Moreover, when you do get a viable clone, it may not turn out to be much like its parent in anything but its genes. Rainbow and cc have different coloring, for example, since the coats of calicos are determined partly by genes and partly by random molecular changes during development. Temperament is also variable. "The fallacy is that cloning provides a duplicate," says the Humane Society's Pacelle. Concedes Westhusin: "This is not a resurrection."

Even if it were possible to create an exact genetic stencil of a lost pooch or kitty, that doesn't mean it's a good idea. Given that more than 5 million unwanted cats are destroyed each year, it's hard to justify spending tens of thousands of dollars to clone a new one. Why not just adopt?

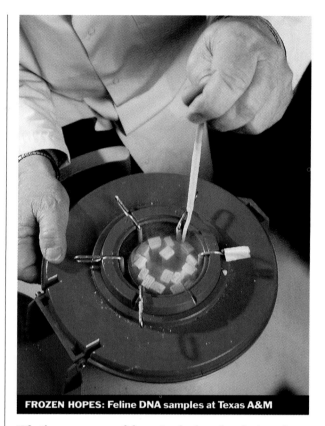

FROZEN HOPES: Feline DNA samples at Texas A&M

What's more, some of the animals cloned so far have been plagued by fatal heart and lung defects in infancy.

Cloning advocates counter that the frailty of clones will be overcome as the technology improves and that the relatively small number of new cloned pets would have little effect on the stray population. What's more, they argue, cloning has scientific applications. Clones could provide a line of identical animals for lab research, for instance, allowing scientists to conduct experiments without the genetic variability that can confound results.

To critics, who view cc as an ethical dry run for human cloning, such arguments seem like moral fig leaves. As if on cue, Panayiotis Zavos, a retired University of Kentucky professor who has strongly declared he wants to be the first to clone a human, announced shortly after the *Nature* article appeared that he has selected 10 infertile couples and is set to begin work. If you thought cc was hard not to love, wait until you see the first baby. ∎

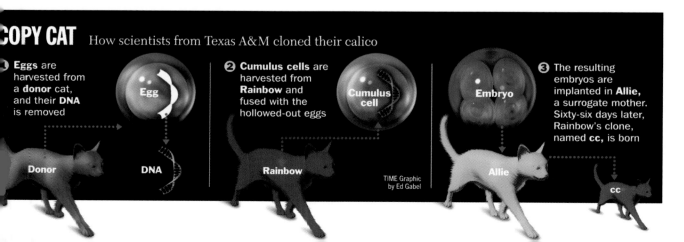

COPY CAT How scientists from Texas A&M cloned their calico

❶ **Eggs** are harvested from a **donor** cat, and their **DNA** is removed

❷ **Cumulus cells** are harvested from **Rainbow** and fused with the hollowed-out eggs

❸ The resulting embryos are implanted in **Allie**, a surrogate mother. Sixty-six days later, Rainbow's clone, named **cc**, is born

Egg

Donor

DNA

Cumulus cell

Rainbow

Embryo

Allie

cc

TIME Graphic by Ed Gabel

Profile

Meet the New Boss

A study of the running ability of *Tyrannosaurus rex,* reported in March in the journal *Nature,* suggests that every boy's favorite dinosaur wasn't quite the speeding predator we once thought. Researchers found that *T. rex* (as imagined in an early 20th century painting, top) was too massive to sprint like the giant-size cheetah it

SIC 'EM! The new portrait of *T. rex,* bottom, differs in many ways from an earlier view of the dinosaur, top

appears to be in the *Jurassic Park* movies. Its top speed was a Sunday-drive 25 m.p.h., not a blistering 45.

The new speed estimate is just the latest in a series of revisions made over the past decade or so, as the fossil record has grown. In our current profile of *T. Rex,* (as seen in the bottom painting), the 42-ft.-long, 14,000-lb. toothy predator does not stand upright, with its tail near the ground for stability; instead, the beast balances its weight over its hips like a seesaw. The dinosaur's nostrils have been repositioned as well: closer to the end of its snout rather than its eyes. Scientists now believe *T. rex* was closer to today's birds than to other dinosaurs of its time; some think juveniles may have been covered with feathers.

SAFE Before and after photographs of the conjoined twins record a surgical triumph

Separated After Birth

Following a 22-hr. operation in Los Angeles in August, a pair of year-old Guatemalan sisters, Maria Teresa and Maria de Jesus Quiej-Alvarez, who were joined at the skull and faced different directions, were safely separated. A 50-member team at Mattel Children's Hospital at UCLA worked around the clock to divide the shared skull and untangle the blood vessels that connected them. Born to Alba Leticia Alvarez, 22, and Wenceslao Quiej Lopez, 21, a banana packer, the girls, whose development before the surgery was normal, are expected to make a full recovery.

Pluto's Playmate

Caltech astronomers Michael Brown and Chadwick Trujillo announced on Oct. 7 that they had located the largest body found in the solar system since Pluto's discovery 72 years ago. Below is an artist's impression of the icy object 2002 LM60, dubbed Quaoar (for a Native American god). Quaoar is about 800 miles (1,300 km) in diameter, half the size of Pluto. Like Pluto, Quaoar dwells in the Kuiper belt, a debris field of comet-like bodies extending 7 billion miles beyond Neptune's orbit. Quaoar is about 4 billion miles (6.5 billion km) from Earth, more than 1 billion miles farther away than Pluto.

Suicide of the Leviathans

It was a summertime saga that gripped the nation: just as the sun rose over the languid beaches of Cape Cod on July 29, strollers were astonished to see surprise

MOVE IT! Rescuers push a pilot whale out to sea

visitors. Lying helplessly in shallows near the town of Dennis, Mass., like so many black boulders, were 55 grounded pilot whales (which are, in fact, large dolphins). Although nine of the whales soon died or had to be put down (with injections of sodium pentothal), rescuers were able to push 46 others out to sea.

But the feel-good story quickly turned bad. During the night, the whales, all dutifully tagged in the morning, beached themselves again, in a salt marsh 25 miles away. By the time good seamaritans got to

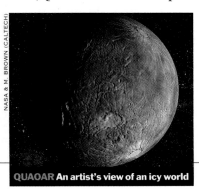

QUAOAR An artist's view of an icy world

Image

Armed Apes

In a major discovery in animal behavior, a team of Harvard University biological anthropologists observed a group of chimpanzees in Uganda in which the males of the group used tools—sticks— to beat the females.

Until now, devising tools to inflict pain and death seemed to be something only humans did. Some animals do use tools: chimps use sticks and stones for all sorts of purposes. But no one before now had ever seen an ape use a stick to beat another ape.

them, six of the animals were dead and nine others had such weak heartbeats that scientists knew they would not make it. Even those that could be refloated soon returned to shore, oblivious to the frantically splashing rescuers trying to shoo them off. By evening, all the pilot whales—mostly females, some of them pregnant—were dead. Scientists could not say why the mammals beached themselves.

Send in the Roborats

Physiologists at the State University of New York Downstate Medical Center in Brooklyn have created remotely piloted rodents that navigate complex terrain at the will of controllers who are more than 500 yards away. Wearing tiny backpacks equipped with radio transmitters and miniature TV cameras, the rats could someday be

sent into a collapsed building to find survivors, say the scientists, or into a minefield to sniff out danger.

The rat controllers issue their instructions by tapping a keyboard that sends signals via radio waves to electrodes implanted in the animal's brain: a mild jolt to neurons that sense the right whiskers means "turn right"; a zap to the left-whisker neurons means "go left." Rodents away!

HOW TO WIRE UP A RODENT

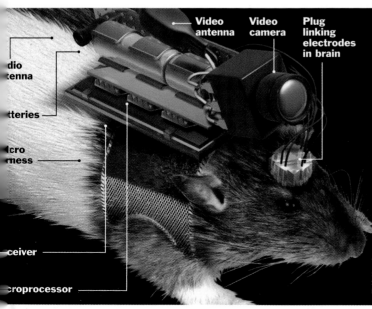

Video antenna **Video camera** **Plug linking electrodes in brain**

dio tenna

tteries

cro rness

ceiver

croprocessor

To steer a roborat by remote control, scientists rely on classic behavioral conditioning. First they implant electrodes in clumps of rat-brain cells that govern whisker sensation and pleasure. When human controllers want the rat to turn left, they beam a signal that triggers a mild electric shock to the left-whisker cells. If the rat responds by turning left, it's rewarded with stimulation of the pleasure cells. A right turn is signaled by a pulse to the right-whisker cells. No signal means the rat should go straight

Rat's brain

Pleasure center

Left-whisker area

Electrodes

Right-whisker area

TIME Diagram by Ed Gabel

Source: Sanjiv Talwar, State University of New York Downstate Medical Center

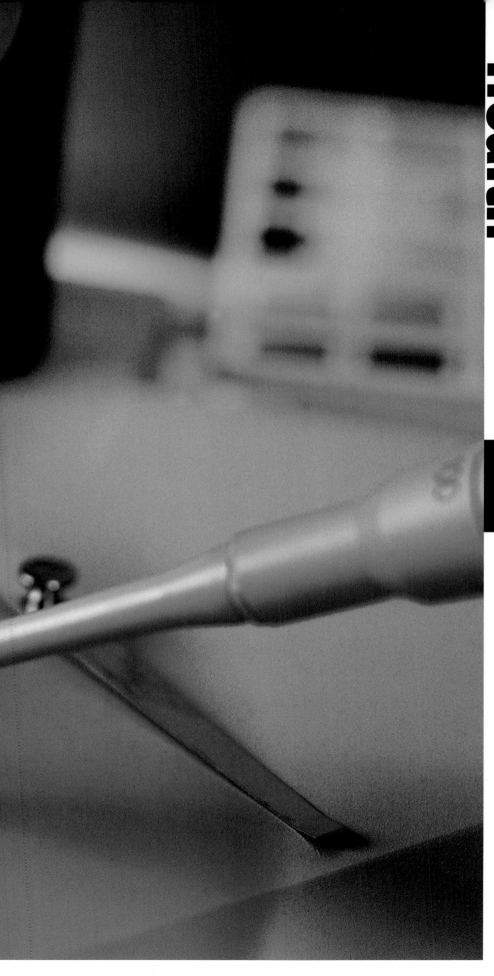

Health

Freezing Human Eggs, Scientists Seek New Ways to Aid Conception

Since 1998, some 40 babies around the world have been born from frozen eggs, raising hopes that the process may someday become a real alternative for women who want to get pregnant after their most fertile years have passed. Unlike embryo freezing, a technique that has already produced thousands of children, egg freezing doesn't require that women choose the baby's father years in advance. At left, human eggs are treated with a cryoprotectant, transferred by pipette to a tiny copper grid and then frozen in liquid nitrogen. Though promising, the process has a low success rate so far, and scientists say more research is in order.

HORMONE THERAPY: THE QUANDARY

A study finds hormone-replacement therapy may be harmful

SUSAN PIERRES, A MIAMI PHOTOJOURNALIST WHO JUST turned 60, is confused and angry. Ten years ago, when she was approaching menopause, her doctor started her on hormone-replacement therapy, or HRT. "I didn't have any symptoms," she recalls, "but he recommended it for general well-being, bones and heart." Many years and pills later, her gynecologist suggested that perhaps it was time to stop. After all, there had been reports that HRT might increase a woman's risk of breast cancer, a disease that had afflicted Pierres' mother and aunt. She turned to several other physicians for advice. They couldn't seem to agree. Then, in the summer of 2002, a major study showed that taking HRT for years at a stretch isn't such a great idea after all.

Should Pierres believe these latest results or go back to her doctor for an explanation? Which doctor? She's not eager to get off hormones. "You feel it is your last vestige of youth. What if my skin turns scaly and my hair falls out?" she worries. "These are complicated matters. People like me don't know where to go or whom to listen to."

Whom indeed. For decades, millions of women like Pierres have been told that HRT is a veritable fountain of youth. It kept the skin supple, held back heart disease, boosted old and brittle bones and might even have staved off senile dementia. More than 40% of all women in the U.S. start some form of HRT in their menopause years. Many of them continue well into their 70s and 80s, convinced that the little pills give them a youthful glow. Like

latter-day Ponce de Leóns, however, these women are watching their dream of eternal youth fade away. A large, federally funded clinical trial, part of a group of studies called the Women's Health Initiative (WHI), definitively showed for the first time that the hormones in question—estrogen and progestin—are not the age-defying wonder drugs everyone thought they were. Moreover, the results,

Alternatives to Hormone Replacement: What Doctors Recomm

STROKE: Reduce blood pressure—and relax

BREAST CANCER: Self-ex

made public in July, proved that taking these hormones together for more than a few years actually increases a woman's risk of developing potentially deadly cardiovascular problems and invasive breast cancer, among other things.

Yes, there are caveats. The WHI wasn't designed to look at short-term use during menopause, for instance. But the principal message is this: taking estrogen and progestin for years in the hope of preventing a heart attack or stroke can no longer be considered a valid medical strategy. The WHI findings were so striking that the study was stopped three years short of its scheduled completion, and the formal scientific report was released a week early.

The phones immediately started ringing. Women across the U.S. began calling their doctors, their mothers, their daughters, their friends. Are you still taking your pills? Do you think plant-based hormones are any better? Physicians scrambled to keep up. The American College of Obstetrics and Gynecology created a task force to rethink its guidelines on HRT.

That's going to be a tough job, for the issue is complicated. The WHI study looked at the most popular brand of estrogen and progestin, which is called Prempro and is made by Wyeth. Technically speaking, the WHI findings do not apply to other products. Some doctors have speculated that lower-dose hormones or estrogen-progestin patches and creams might somehow avoid some of the risks associated with Prempro. That has yet to be proved. Even so-called natural hormones (derived from plants) aren't necessarily risk free.

There is also a good chance that certain estrogen-like

BY THE NUMBERS: The Women's Health Initiative study involves 160,00 post-menopausal women

compounds may be designed that will capture all the hormone's benefits without any of its risks. One such drug, raloxifene, has been shown to prevent bone fractures, so far without increasing a woman's risk of breast cancer. But a number of women suffer hot flashes and even blood clots while on raloxifene, making it unlikely to replace estrogen completely.

Women should not panic if they are using HRT for short-term relief of menopausal miseries. For in a strange sort of way, the study brings HRT back to the basics, doing what it always did best—alleviating intense hot flashes, night sweats and mood swings during the limited period in which they occur. "Estrogens," said Dr. Howard Judd of UCLA, part of the WHI team, "are still the best, and in many ways the only, way of treating menopause."

The tricky part is going to be figuring out just how long women need to stay on HRT, how best to wean them off the treatment and then how to protect them from osteoporosis and other ravages of age without resorting to old-fashioned hormones. "The world of menopause management," said Dr. Wulf Utian of the North American Menopause Society, "has just become a lot more complex."

And part of that complexity is dealing with the emotional attachment that some women have to their HRT regimen. Many like the way they look and feel on the stuff. Change is scary. And that, perhaps, is why Susan Pierres, the angry and frustrated Miami photojournalist, was taking her time before parting with her pills. ■

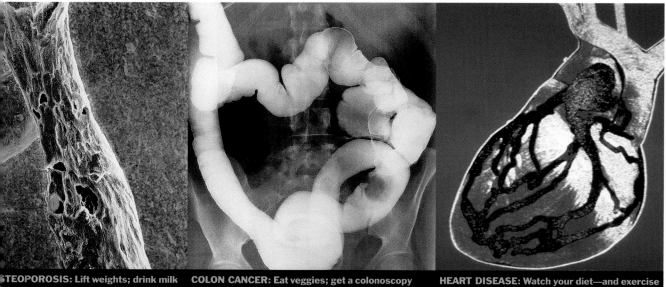

OSTEOPOROSIS: Lift weights; drink milk   **COLON CANCER:** Eat veggies; get a colonoscopy   **HEART DISEASE:** Watch your diet—and exercise

THE YEAR IN MEDICINE

An A to Z Guide

APPETITE:
A hormone can
reduce it

From anxiety to viruses, a roundup of good
news, bad news and breakthroughs in health

Anxiety

Researchers have made significant progress in recent years in nailing down the underlying science of anxiety disorder, which afflicts 19 million Americans. Among the findings: there is a genetic component to anxiety (some people are born worriers); brain scans can reveal differences in the way normal people and patients who suffer from anxiety disorders react

ANXIOUS?
You're not alone

LWA—STEPHEN WELSTEAD—CORBIS

to danger signals; and the root of an anxiety disorder may not be the threat that triggers it but rather a breakdown in the mechanism that keeps the anxiety response from careening out of control.

Appetite Suppressant

No, it isn't a fantasy; it's more like a dream come true. A simple hormone, long thought to play an obscure function in the pancreas, turns out to be a powerful appetite suppressant—the body's way of telling the brain it's time to push the plate away. The hormone's name is PYY_{3-36}, but scientists dubbed it "the fullness hormone."

When volunteers in London were injected with PYY, led to a buffet table and invited to eat their fill, they voluntarily consumed one-third fewer calories than those given a placebo. Scientists don't know the side effects of PYY yet, nor can they put it into pill form. But it holds real promise in the fight to understand and treat obesity.

Autism

An unexplained increase in the number of children who receive a diagnosis of autism has spurred research into the mysterious disease. The brain scans below are part of a breakthrough study that showed the autistic brain at work.

Scientists had long believed that people with autism did not register faces of loved ones as special—that, in the words of a prominent brain expert, they view their own mother's face as the equivalent of a paper cup. But the bottom three scans

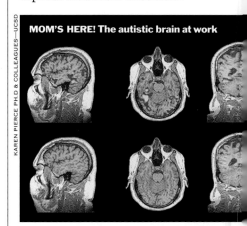

MOM'S HERE! The autistic brain at work

KAREN PIERCE PH.D & COLLEAGUES—UCSD

show an autistic brain reacting to the faces of strangers, while the top three show the same brain reacting to loved ones—and lighting up like an explosion of Roman candles.

Another provocative finding: the components that may contribute to autism, far more than autism itself, tend to run in families.

NICK KELSH FOR TIME (3)

BOTOX: A new wrinkle in cosmetics

Bipolar Disorder

Once known as manic depression, bipolar disorder seems to be showing up in children at an increasing rate, surprising mental-health professionals. Until recently, the illness was thought of as the province of luckless adults. But the average age of onset has fallen in a single generation from the early 30s to the late teens. Victims of the disease have an alcoholism and drug-abuse rate triple that of the rest of the population, and a suicide rate that may approach 20%.

DIETING? Carbohydrates are key

DAVID WOODS—CORBIS

The good news about bipolar disorder: a genetic connection may help diagnosis; new drugs are capable of leveling the manic peaks; and new behavioral therapies are helping patients cope.

Botox

Are you sufficiently bothered by wrinkles to stick needles into your face? That's the question millions of Americans were asking themselves when the Food and Drug Administration approved the use of botox injections to fight facial wrinkles. Botox is short for botulinim toxin, the substance that causes botulism, a sometimes fatal form of food poisoning. But in small doses, it merely interrupts nerve impulses to muscles in the face—and goodbye, wrinkles!

Critics say the treatment leaves one stone-faced, and doctors point out it can't help most wrinkles caused by age, but now that the FDA has given its approval for the cosmetic use of botox, its use is expected to skyrocket.

Carbohydrates and Diet

Thirty years ago, Dr. Robert Atkins argued that low-fat diets, which are typically high in carbohydrates, are bad, and that low-carbohydrate diets, which often contain high levels of fat, are good. In short: eat more steaks and less bread.

Reluctantly, mainstream obesity experts are now saying the Atkins approach merits serious study, while the low-fat paradigm is under question. It turns out that not all fats are bad for you. Those found in fish, nuts and some vegetables may increase your chances of living a good long life. Nor are all diets that are low in fat necessarily healthy. But most diet experts still recommend a balanced diet that is low in calories and includes a good helping of exercise on the side.

Human Guinea Pigs

Over the past three years, more than 60 institutions, including several very prestigious research centers, have been criticized by the U.S. government for failing to protect human subjects adequately

GUINEA PIGS: An atom bomb test, 1951

BETTMANN CORBIS

in clinical trials. As such trials continue to involve more Americans, bills were introduced in Congress to protect research subjects, and the federal Office for Human Research Protections is rewriting its rules. A word of advice: Never sign up for a clinical trial without thoroughly reviewing its sponsor.

Kava

This relative of the pepper plant grows on Polynesian islands and is famous for the dreamy state of mind it induces. Kava fans claim it can ease anything from anxiety and insomnia to menopause side effects. Stressed-out Americans spend more than $50 million on the

KAVA: Caveats

GILBERT GRANT—PHOTO RESEARCHERS

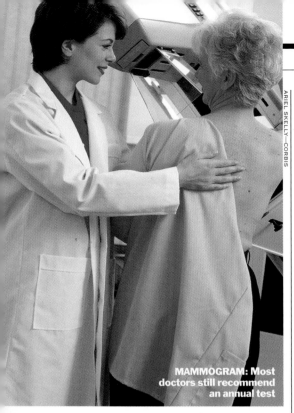

MAMMOGRAM: Most doctors still recommend an annual test

stuff. But as reports of liver damage piled up, the FDA issued a kava alert: Don't take kava every day for more than four weeks straight, and don't exceed the standard dosage.

Listeria

Scientists have known for years that a group of tiny bacteria called listeria can cause illness in animals. But it wasn't until the early 1980s that studies confirmed that humans can develop listeriosis as well. For most of us, a listeria infection is not a major

MARIJUANA: Helps pain, but can harm

problem. But an infection can be quite serious for anybody with a weakened immune system. That includes the very old, the very young, cancer patients and those who are HIV positive.

In October, a food processor voluntarily recalled more than 27 million pounds of meat to prevent a listeria outbreak. To protect yourself:
• Cook beef, pork and poultry thoroughly and be sure to wash raw vegetables well before eating
• Keep uncooked meats separate from vegetables and other foods
• Avoid, if you are at high risk, hot dogs, luncheon meats, soft cheeses, pâté and meat spreads.

Mammograms

The long-simmering debate over the value of women's getting routine mammograms to detect breast cancer flared up again in 2002 when experts questioned whether the test has been sufficiently proved to save lives. Trials in the 1960s showed that the breast exam reduces the risk of dying from cancer as much as 30%. But two Danish scientists said the early studies were flawed, and that there is no real benefit to mammograms. Proponents agreed the test is not perfect—it misses some 10% of breast cancers—but strongly urged women to continue to take it.

There is good news about breast cancer: new tools of treatment can destroy tumors while sparing more breast tissue and without reducing the chances of survival. And doctors are finding new methods of delivering lethal radiation that reduce treatment time and target tumors better.

Marijuana

The politics of pot can be, well, disorienting. A number of ballot initiatives in favor of slackening anti-pot laws went down to defeat in the fall election, yet a TIME/CNN poll found that a whopping 80% of Americans are in favor of making pot available for medical use.

The science of marijuana is a bit less confusing. Reseachers haven't found a conclusive link to cancer, and pot doesn't seem to retard sexual drive, but they have found that pot increases the work of the heart, is more irritating to the lungs than tobacco and may reduce the number and quality of sperm. Research hasn't yet proved that pot helps relieve pains caused by glaucoma, nausea or surgery.

Migraine

A revolutionary view of extreme headaches now regards these attacks as serious, biologically based disorders on a par with epilepsy or Alzheimer's disease.

When 60 scientists from 32 countries gathered for the biennial

MIGRAINE: New drugs can help

symposium of the Migraine Trust, the excitement centered on a study showing that the anti-epilepsy drug topiramate significantly reduces both the occurrence and duration of migraines. While more research on the drug is needed, a new class of drugs called triptans is available that offers significant relief to most who get migraines.

Nicotine Lollipops

It began as a well-intentioned effort to help people lick smoking. The idea: give tobacco smokers something to suck on that would satisfy

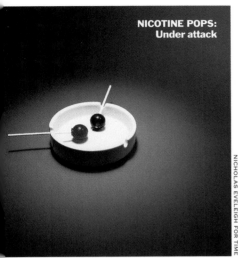

NICOTINE POPS: Under attack

their nicotine cravings without all the health problems associated with smoking. *Voilà!*—the nicotine lollipop! Unlike such earlier nicotine substitutes as patches and chewing gums, the suckers come in appealing flavors like Very Berry and Lemon Lime and are shaped like lollipops and gummi bears. And that's what put them in the crosshairs of antismoking activists, who didn't cotton to the notion of nicotine disguised as candy.

In the spring, prompted by an article in the *Wall Street Journal* about the booming sales of nicotine lollipops with names like Nicostop and Likatine, the FDA banned the pops, which seemed to pack the same buzz as a smoke. A former user reported that after sucking on one of the lollipops for a few minutes and then putting it aside, he found himself thinking about it all the time.

Smallpox Redux?

Just two decades after it was declared gone for good, this deadly scourge is back—in our fears if not in fact. Smallpox in the hands of terrorists could be a far more devastating bioweapon than anthrax. There is no effective treatment for the disease, and because routine vaccination was halted in 1972, even a single case could spread like wildfire. Officially, the only remaining

sources of the virus are small quantities kept at two secure labs in the U.S. and Russia. Experts believe, however, that Iraq, North Korea and Russia may have secretly pursued weapons research that involved smallpox. Erring on the side of caution, the White House ordered several million doses of the vaccine, to be given to soldiers and emergency personnel—if necessary.

What to do if more are needed? In March, U.S. officials announced that 15.4 million freeze-dried doses left over from the 1970s could be diluted fivefold—stretching the stockpile to more than 75 million doses—and still remain potent. Meanwhile, a French drug firm

SMALLPOX: Getting vaccinations in 1946

offered to share a long-forgotten cache of 85 million more doses.

Vegetarianism

At the International Congress of Vegetarian Nutrition at Loma Linda (Calif.) University in the spring, researchers announced some encouraging findings for those who eschew meat: vegetarian seniors have a lower death rate and use less medication than meat-eating seniors; compared with meat eaters, vegetarians

have a healthier total intake of fats and cholesterol but a less healthy intake of good fatty acids. However, one study indicated that the low-protein diets typical of vegetarianism reduce calcium absorption and may have a negative impact on skeletal health. Doctors advise vegetarians to make sure they get enough protein, vitamins and essential fatty acids.

West Nile Virus

Borne by mosquitoes, the virus first reported in the U.S. in New York City in 1999 is believed to have reached every state in the continental U.S. by the fall of 2002, except for five states in the West. By mid-August, seven fatalities had been reported in Louisiana. The federal Centers for Disease Control and Prevention announced that 3,698 cases had caused 212 deaths by late November. While work on a vaccine to ward off West Nile is promising, the CDC says we will be watching out for skeeters again in 2003.

WEST NILE: A deadly year

HEALTH 147

Photograph by Paul Kolnik

The Arts

A Plus-Size Hit Turns
The Great White Way
Into a Day-Glo Rainbow

For its latest musical smash, Broadway headed for an unlikely destination: 1960s Baltimore, by way of offbeat filmmaker John Waters' 1988 movie *Hairspray*. Audiences loved it, and critics worked themselves into a lather of metaphor: as hefty Tracy Turnblad, star Marissa Jaret Winokur, left, was "a buoyant fireplug." As her even heftier mom, Harvey Fierstein *(Torch Song Trilogy)*, center, had a voice "like a dump truck in fourth gear"...or was it "a buzzsaw"? The sets celebrated "fantasyland bad tasteless-ness" (that's a rave). And the hairstyles? "They could make Marie Antoinette want to go into show business."

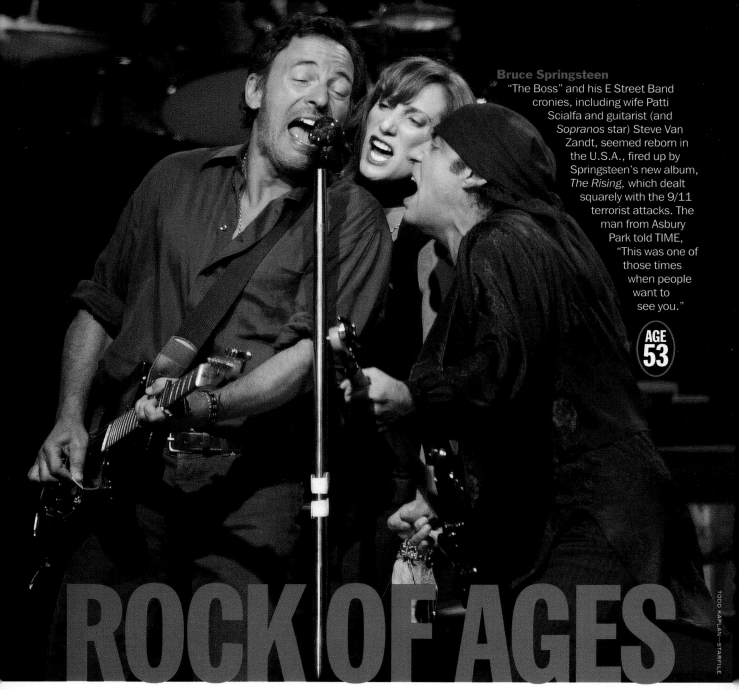

Bruce Springsteen
"The Boss" and his E Street Band cronies, including wife Patti Scialfa and guitarist (and *Sopranos* star) Steve Van Zandt, seemed reborn in the U.S.A., fired up by Springsteen's new album, *The Rising*, which dealt squarely with the 9/11 terrorist attacks. The man from Asbury Park told TIME, "This was one of those times when people want to see you."

AGE 53

TODD KAPLAN—STARFILE

ROCK OF AGES

Dinosaurs? Nostalgia acts? No way. Battle-scarred rockers hit the road and prove Neil Young was right: Better to burn out than to fade away

HOLD THE JOKES, FOLKS—WE'VE HEARD THEM ALL. YES, Keith Richards' face seems to be all seams. Yes, a young Mick Jagger once said he couldn't imagine strutting around a stage singing *Satisfaction* at age 40. Yes, a young Pete Townshend once famously vowed, "Hope I die before I get old." Some colleagues of the veteran rockers pictured here achieved that dubious goal, including Townshend's Who mate, drummer Keith Moon, who died at 31 in 1978. But in 2002, as a posse of stars from rock's greatest era hit stages around the world, they proved that their music was still vital. This was no parade of past-their-prime pre-Madonnas: in city after city, fans and critics alike hailed concerts by the Rolling Stones, Paul Mc-

Cartney, the Who, Bob Dylan and Bruce Springsteen as bursting with vigor, daring and sass. Dylan, said the *New Yorker*, "just happens to be at the peak of his career."

What keeps them going? Cynics say it's the money, but anyone remotely familiar with the financial status of these artists knows they are already wealthy. (FORTUNE magazine devoted a September cover story to the vast Rolling Stones empire.) Part of it may be a taste for adulation: Jagger has said that the adrenaline high he gets from performing is more addictive than any drug. Call us corny, but we suspect these musicians are simply living by the age-old code of true show people: they are reveling in the sheer joy of their gifts—and the buzz of sharing it with others. ∎

Paul McCartney
Thirty-eight years after the Beatles first conquered America, Sir Paul won raves for his live show, which offered classics never played live before, like *She's Leaving Home* from the *Sgt. Pepper* album. Paul helped Queen Elizabeth celebrate her jubilee, then did a spot of celebrating of his own: the widower wed anti-land mine activist Heather Mills in June at a castle in Ireland.

AGE 60

AGE 61

AGE 58

AGE 57

Bob Dylan
It's hard to recall that the gifted songwriter who turned folk into rock was once a recluse. For years, Dylan has been on what fans call "The Never-ending Tour." Traveling by bus, he plays state fairs, rodeos, arts centers—anywhere there's a stage—as many as 20 nights a month.

The Who
Singer Roger Daltrey, left, and songwriter Pete Townshend reacted to the sudden death of bassist John Entwistle on the eve of a major tour by calling off two shows, then—what else?—hitting the road. Fans deemed them rejuvenated, even if smart-alecks dubbed it the "Who's Left?" tour.

Rolling Stones
Models of consistency, the Stones mount gigantic tours, complete with silly photo-op kick-offs—like this year's blimp—every few years. But in 2002 Mick Jagger, Keith Richards & Co. regained their edge by playing concerts in not only giant arenas but also smaller halls and even tiny nightclubs. The critical consensus: better than ever.

AGE 61

AGE 59

AGE 55

AGE 59

MICHAEL BRITO—STARFILE

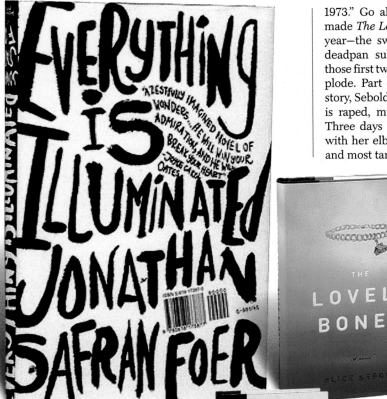

BOUND FOR GLORY

Three young writers make 2002 a memorable year for new fiction

REPORTS OF THE DEATH OF READING IN AN ONLINE AGE may have been exaggerated. When Oprah Winfrey gave up her influential TV book club in 2002, other shows were only too eager to launch their own printfest kaffeeklatsches. And the appearance in 2002 of powerful—and high-selling—first novels by a trio of young writers ensured that Barnes & Noble might just survive for another quarter or two. TIME's reviews:

THE LOVELY BONES, by Alice Sebold (Little, Brown; 336 pages). "My name was Salmon, like the fish: first name, Susie. I was 14 when I was murdered on December 6,

1973." Go ahead, read it again. Almost everything that made *The Lovely Bones* the breakout fiction debut of the year—the sweetness, the humor, the kicky rhythm, the deadpan suburban gothic—is right there, packed into those first two sentences, under pressure and waiting to explode. Part coming-of-age tale, part mystery, part ghost story, Sebold's first novel is the tale of an ordinary girl who is raped, murdered and dismembered near her house. Three days later, a neighbor's dog comes trotting home with her elbow in its mouth. This is horror at its darkest and most tantalizing, and as first chapters go, it's a knockout. The second chapter tops it.

What happens to little girls after they die? They go to heaven—and that's exactly what Susie does. In *The Lovely Bones* (an exquisite corpse of a title), heaven is a warm, grassy place. But when Susie turns her attention back to earth, she watches as the shock waves of her death spread slow-motion havoc among her family and friends. She watches dispassionately as her killer carefully disperses her body parts (the hunt for the murderer gives the book a fierce narrative energy).

Sebold knows what it is to be haunted. In 1981, as a freshman in college, she was beaten and raped by a stranger. The trauma left her with ghosts that needed exorcising, and it wasn't until 1996, after two earlier failed novels and half of a third, that inspiration finally arrived. She wrote the first 15 pages of *The Lovely Bones* in a single, unexpected rush that left her shaken. But two years into the novel, she felt she had to take a break to write a memoir, *Lucky*, a searingly honest account of her rape.

"I felt as if I had a story of my own that was bearing down on me in such a way that it would infuse and therefore ruin Susie's story," says Sebold, who is 39 and lives near Los Angeles with her husband Glen David Gold, also a writer. "I wanted Susie's story to be a novel." It is. *The Lovely Bones* is free of any veiled autobiographical traces, and that's both a personal and an artistic triumph. And a hit with readers: *The Lovely Bones* became the year's No. 1 novel, outselling books by Stephen King and Tom Clancy.

EVERYTHING IS ILLUMINATED, by Jonathan Safran Foer (Houghton Mifflin; 276 pages), is a very funny book about very tragic times, and it's just a little bit nervous about being so funny. It is written as a duet for two voices. One belongs to Foer (or his fictional alter ego of the same name), who relates the history of Trachimbrod, the East European village where his ancestors lived. Trachimbrod is a lyrical, fairy-tale creation, a Yiddish idyll of the *Fiddler on the Roof* variety. Perchov, the novel's other, more successfully realized narrator, tells a different tale. A would-be hipster, he acts as a translator when Foer takes a trip to Ukraine to find present-day Trachimbrod. Bluff, gruff and unflappable, he

SEBOLD: She interrupted a novel on rape to write a memoir of rape

KRISTINA LOGGIA—CORBIS OUTLINE

YOU SHALL KNOW OUR VELOCITY, by Dave Eggers (McSweeney's Books; 371 pages). At 32, Eggers is the yeti of American letters: powerful, mysterious, mischievous but (probably) benevolent. Even before the huge success of *A Heartbreaking Work of Staggering Genius*, his moving account of caring for his younger brother after the death of their parents, Eggers was a literary Johnny Appleseed who anted up to found the literary journal *McSweeney's* and its publishing imprint, McSweeney's Books. In 2002 he established a nonprofit center in San Francisco that tutors students in writing. He also slipped into self-imposed obscurity, avoiding the press and staging his readings as cryptic, Andy Kaufman–style happenings. *Velocity* was brought out slyly, in an initial printing of a mere 10,000 copies, available only at alternative bookstores.

Our heroes are Will and Hand, two twentynothing layabouts from Wisconsin who decide to fly around the world for a week, handing out money to strangers. They recently lost a friend in a car accident, and in some way, the trip is an attempt to deal with that loss, as well as with their more generalized sense of aimlessness and anger. Will and Hand ricochet unsteadily from country to country in picaresque fashion, drinking, bickering, not sleeping, thrusting wads of cash at startled strangers, staying just ahead of boredom but just behind the sense of happiness and belonging they're sure awaits them in the next strip bar or hotel lobby or wherever.

JANA LEON—CORBIS OUTLINE

FOER: A virtuoso with language, he also takes typography for a spin

writes in broken English: "I dig Negroes, particularly Michael Jackson. I dig to disseminate very much currency at famous nightclubs in Odessa."

In alternating chapters, the two voices come at the plot from both ends at once, Foer moving forward in time through Trachimbrod's history, and Perchov searching backward for it. They also share themes: the maddening bonds of family, the power of memory, the importance of lies and jokes. The stories collide when the searchers learn the dread secret of how the dreamy little village met its end in World War II.

A certified wunderkind at 25, Foer spares no expense with his typographical special effects: italics, CAPITAL LETTERS, onomatopoeia and song lyrics. But under it all there's a funny, moving, unsteady, deeply felt novel about the dangers of confronting the past and the redemption that comes with laughing at it. The compelling tale became a best seller, and Foer, a total unknown to most readers before its publication, scored one of the strongest fiction debuts in years.

JAMES LEYNSE—CORBIS SABA

EGGERS: The writer as trickster, he shuns publicity (in a public way)

Eggers' strengths as a writer are real: his dialogue is funny and pitch-perfect; his prose has a stream-water clarity. At their best, Will and Hand, like Vladimir and Estragon, have genuine existential pathos; at their worst they're a little jejune, a pair of Holden Caulfields railing at the phonies. But there's genius here, and the book deserves our forgiveness and our respect, as does Eggers himself. After all, who is doing more, single-handedly and single-mindedly, for American writing, than this yeti? ∎

Jennifer Aniston
The Good Girl

Ask David Caruso: the transition from TV to the big screen is the roughest commute in L.A. But *Friends* star Jennifer Aniston—who failed to ignite in earlier made-to-measure movies like *Picture Perfect* and *Office Space*—finally got it right by playing against type. Aniston, 33, won raves for her performance in *The Good Girl,* a dark independent comedy, in which she played a small-town Texas woman with a dead-end job who gets herself into a fix between her stoned-out husband and a much younger man. *Friends* fans knew Mrs. Brad Pitt had excellent comic timing, but her breakthrough role revealed an actress of surprising subtlety and range.

Vin Diesel
XXX

For the past decade, Hollywood has been desperately trying to pump some testosterone into the lucrative but ailing action genre. With Arnold Schwarzenegger and Sly Stallone nearing 60, the studios have resorted to subbing in skinny guys like Keanu Reeves and Nicolas Cage. Now a new savior is on the horizon. Vin Diesel is tough, stocky and tawny, with muscles like Adonis and a voice like Bea Arthur. Diesel's star was born in the 2001 surprise street-racing hit *The Fast and the Furious;* he scored again with this year's *XXX,* playing Xander Cage, an un–James Bond for guys like Diesel himself—the tattooed with 'tude.

Naomi Watts
The Ring

The gifted Brit who grew up in Australia has been on the cusp of stardom for years now. But even though Naomi Watts' 2001 turn as a shady lady in David Lynch's *Mulholland Drive* received glowing reviews, few saw it. This year was different: as Rachel Keller, a smart, flawed journalist and single mom trying to save her son and herself from a killer videotape, Watts was gutsy and game in one of the year's most unexpected hits. Now the Watts bandwagon is rolling: after *The Ring,* Watts, 34, will appear in four other new releases, including *The Kelly Gang,* in which she stars opposite fellow Aussie (and new beau), 23-year-old Heath Ledger.

BUMPER CROP

Hooray for Hollywood! The star-making machinery was working overtime in 2002, churning out captivating new faces for the silver screen—and the box-office green

Tobey Maguire
Spider-Man

Who was that masked man? Serious movie fans (no, that's not an oxymoron) had admired Tobey Maguire's work in a remarkable skein of high-end films: *The Ice Storm* (1997), *Pleasantville* (1998), *The Cider House Rules* (1999) and *Wonder Boys* (2000). In these troubled-teen roles, his performances were enigmatic and haunting—hardly swaggering leading-man turns wherein he saves the day and gets the girl. But in 2002 Tobey donned the costume of comic-book superhero Spider-Man, and—*shazzam!*—he saved New York City, got Kirsten Dunst and became a superstar. By year's end *Spider-Man* had become the fifth highest-grossing film in Hollywood history and had set sales records on its release in DVD form. As for the star's newfound celebrity? "It's kind of surreal," he told TIME. Get used to it, Tobey.

Cedric the Entertainer
Barbershop

Cedric Kyles dubbed himself "the Entertainer" back in his early night-club days, when he would fill out his comedy act with a little hoofing and singing. The St. Louis–born comic had been a hit with nightclub audiences since the early '90s and vaulted to fame as one of the self-proclaimed "Original Kings of Comedy," the four-man black troupe whose hilarious acts were chronicled in a 2000 Spike Lee documentary.

In 2002 Cedric, 38, took another giant step, starring in the gentle comedy *Barbershop*. The film, which portrays daily life in an African-American community, crossed over to tickle white funnybones as well and earned $80 million at the box office. And, yes, that was Cedric who memorably drenched his date in a hilarious 2002 beer ad.

Reese Witherspoon
Sweet Home Alabama

You know you've made it in Hollywood when the ads for your latest movie feature only your fabulous face. So when the posters for the romantic-comedy hit *Sweet Home Alabama* offered just a close-up of a now familiar mug, it was clear that Reese Witherspoon had arrived. There's an even more accurate barometer, of course: the star with the subversively perky grin and the don't-mess-with-me chin, who made a splash in 2001's *Legally Blonde,* will take home as much as 15 million when she reprises her role as Elle Woods in the hit comedy's sequel, *Red, White and Blonde.*

Salma Hayek
Frida

Talk about a catfight: Salma Hayek had to beat out both Madonna and Jennifer Lopez to bring the Technicolor life of Mexican artist Frida Kahlo to the screen. But the Mexican-born Hayek, 34, once a soap-opera star, took on the role of producer and won the race. Hiring Julie Taymor (Broadway's *The Lion King*) to direct and picking a strong cast that included boyfriend Ed Norton, Ashley Judd and Geoffrey Rush, Hayek hoped to hit a home run—and elevate herself above the so-so reviews she had garnered in *Wild Wild West* (1999) and *Fools Rush In* (1997). Ironically, she may have both failed and succeeded. Though *Frida* wasn't a huge hit, Hayek's new visibility as a can-do producer/actress promises to make her a hot commodity in Hollywood for years to come.

Profile

American Gothic

TV's most surprising hit of the year: *The Osbournes,* MTV's "reality sitcom." Starring Ozzy Osbourne, the former front man (i.e., wild man) of British heavy-metal band Black Sabbath, his wife Sharon and teenagers Kelly and Jack, the show was expected to provide crucifixes on the doors and enough bleeped-out cursing to give Pat Robertson

OZZIE & CO. "Happy families are all alike ..."

the vapors. And it did. Its brilliance was in its surprising ordinariness: Ozzy puzzling over the satellite-TV remote or struggling to fit liners in the trash bin. The unspoken context of the show's humor is that Ozzy's problems were not always of the garden variety; he often speaks of his substance-abusing past. Now he tells his kids to say no to drugs and use a condom if they have sex.

Riding high after the success of a 13-show spring run, the family got $20 million to return in the fall, but reality knocked on their door with a vengeance when mom Sharon, the family's voice of reason, was diagnosed with colorectal cancer in July. Though the show did go on in the fall, the Osbournes announced it would be their last season on MTV. Even so, ailing Sharon announced plans to host a new TV talk show.

MARK J. TERRILL—AP/WIDE WORLD

OSCAR'S BIG NIGHT Washington and Berry grip and grin

Black Stars Reap Gold

On a night of triumph for African-American actors, the 2002 Oscar Awards for Best Actor and Best Actress were presented to Denzel Washington, 47, and Halle Berry, 35. Berry was the first black actress ever to win the coveted statue; Washington was the first black to receive the Oscar for Best Actor since Sidney Poitier in 1964.

Berry earned the honor for her role as a worn-out waitress in *Monster's Ball.* Washington, often cast as the strong silent hero, was honored for his gritty portrait of a bad guy—a corrupt L. A. cop in *Training Day.* After the 4 hr. 24 min. award show, Washington teased his clearly overwhelmed fellow winner. "She doesn't know where she is," he claimed. "She's gone—she's out there." Berry agreed. "I never thought it would be possible in my lifetime," she said.

White Star Raps Bold

Setting a new record in the fine art of turning from despised and feared rebel to acclaimed star (a process that took Ozzy Osbourne

Roundup

PICTURES BY OKSYNDICATION.COM

LIZA: Michael Jackson and Elizabeth Taylor joined the fragile star and her new hub, David Gest, at their wedding, true Lizapalooza

MARIAH: After her label, Virgin, gave her $28 million to leave, Universal signed her. She released *Charmbracelet* in December

UK PRESS—GETTY IMAGES

Gettin' Down with the Divas

Divas—you gotta love 'em. Especially this year, when one diva after another took a dive: Madonna drew scorn for her acting in a remake of the '70s film *Swept Away.* Britney threw a hissy fit and halted her show mid-concert in Mexico City. Mariah was dumped by her record label and strained to regain her twinkle. And Liza—well, just look at the picture above.

about 15 years), white rap pariah Eminem rocketed to screen stardom with a winning turn in *8 Mile*. Playing (surprise!) a white rapper on the rise in Detroit, his home town, the 30-year-old was praised for his vulnerability, his intensity and his lingual velocity: TIME clocked him spitting out 1,100

EMINEM He scored a hit in his screen debut

words in the 6-min. title song alone. Director Curtis Hanson (*L.A. Confidential*) shrewdly recast the life of Marshall Mathers as a kind of rapper's *Rocky*—and the result was a hit that brought in $51 million on its first weekend alone.

MADONNA: Though few were *Swept Away* by her acting in the film directed by husband Guy Ritchie, Madonna and gal pal Donatella Versace succeeded in luring Chelsea Clinton over to the dark side

BRITNEY: The supervixen, 20, once an oasis of sanity in the ditzy desert of divadom, broke up with Justin Timberlake and said she'd give recording and touring a rest for a while

Image

Treasure Found

When he saw the drawing in April, Sir Timothy Clifford later said, he recognized Michelangelo's line "at a glance." It took three months of scrutiny for scholars to verify that Clifford, director of the National Galleries of Scotland, had discovered the first Michelangelo to be found in America in 26 years in the archives of New York City's Cooper-Hewitt National Design Museum. Among the clues: cherubs that resemble those the master painted on the ceiling of the Sistine Chapel.

Old Star Rejoins Fold

Feeling older? You may when you hear that it's been nine years since David Caruso made waves on ABC's street-smart police procedural, *NYPD Blue*—and made more waves for ditching the show after only one season, aiming for big-screen glory. It didn't quite work out that way, and this fall Caruso returned to the tube as Horatio Caine, the lead investigator in *CSI: Miami*, the first spin-off from CBS's phenomenally popular series about a homicide forensics unit. Joining Caruso was another familiar *Blue* veteran, Kim Delaney.

Thanks to their love affair with the alloy of science and crime, TV viewers could tune into a forensics drama almost every night of the week, starting with the trendsetting *CSI*

and its Miami spawn on CBS; *Crossing Jordan* on NBC; *The Forensics Files* on Court TV, the cable channel's biggest prime-time show ever; and *Autopsy* on HBO. Sure enough, *CSI: Miami* got off to the best start in the ratings for a new show since the debut of *ER* on NBC in 1994.

CARUSO Back in the saddle again

Milestones

Farewell to Britain's Grand Lady, the Feisty, Beloved Queen Mum

One of the most admired royals in history, the woman christened Elizabeth Angela Marguerite Bowes-Lyon in 1900 lived through the entire 20th century. As wife of King George VI, she reigned as Britain's Queen from 1936 to 1952. When her daughter Elizabeth took the throne, the former Queen assumed the role of Queen Mum, which she played with gusto for 50 years. Here we see her in her finest hour, the stern days of World War II, visiting with WRENS (Women's Royal Navy Service). She refused to leave bombed-out London during the Battle of Britain, declaring, "The children won't go without me, I won't leave without the King, and the King will never leave."

John Gotti
1940-2002

He was a throwback to the days of Al Capone and Lucky Luciano, a swaggering, vain Mob boss whose $2,000 suits made him the "Dapper Don." (He framed TIME's 1986 Andy Warhol cover portrait of himself and hung it in his office). But there was no denying his brutality. "He's a murderer, not a folk hero," a prosecuting attorney once had to remind people.

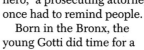

Born in the Bronx, the young Gotti did time for a truck hijacking and attempted manslaughter. He planned the very public murder of Mob boss Paul Castellano in 1985, then took over as capo of the Gambino crime family. He beat racketeering charges in 1987 and 1990, earning a new tag: "the Teflon Don." But in 1992 he was convicted of Castellano's murder, after longtime comrade Sammy (the Bull) Gravano testified against him. Gotti died of cancer in a federal medical center. He was wearing a prison smock.

Ted Williams
1918-2002

How could someone whose nickname was "the Splendid Splinter" be so much larger than life? Ted Williams was a parade of contradictions: a slugger camouflaged in a lean body, a championship fisherman who was known for his impatience, an idol both beloved and scorned by fans in his own ballpark. Born in San Diego, he joined the Red Sox in 1939 at age 20. Cocky and intense, "the Kid" was determined to become the best hitter in the history of baseball. Most fans agree that he reached his goal. Yet impressive as his statistics are—a .344 lifetime batting average, 521 home runs—they would have been much higher if Williams hadn't served as a pilot in both World War II and Korea (where he was John Glenn's wingman).

Williams approached hitting as a science, studying every aspect of the process: bat weight, wind conditions, the strike zone, each pitcher's bag of tricks. The left-handed batter claimed he could see the seams on an incoming fastball—why doubt him? But even in his heyday, Williams' greatness was too often overlooked. When he batted .406 in 1941—he was the last player in baseball to top .400— sportswriters voted the popular Joe DiMaggio the Ameri- can League's Most Valuable Player. Only after retirement were Williams' deeds fully appreciated. At the 1999 All-Star Game at Boston' Fenway Park, the game's best living players mobbed Williams when he threw out the first ball, a crowd of mortals haiing a figure from an age of giants.

Rest in peace? Not Williams. His death was tarnished by a family quarrel over the disposition of his body. But even when that flap is long forgotten, baseball fans will recall the ornery Williams—and come up with new ones.

Ann Landers
1918-2002

One of a kind? Almost. She may have been the world's No. 1 advice columnist, but the woman born Esther (Eppie) Friedman wasn't even the first Ann Landers—she was the second, assuming the alias used by the Chicago Sun-Times for its society-page confidant in 1955. By the 1960s she had updated the genre's musty format, counseling those confused by rapidly changing mores in a brisk, no-nonsense voice. She wasn't even the only Friedman in the advice biz: when twin sister Pauline became competitor Abigail Van Buren, the sisters feuded for years. A job for Ann Landers!

Bill Blass
1922-2002

He was the son of a hardware-store owner, a combat veteran who proudly fought in the Battle of the Bulge, a hardworking chain-smoker who claimed his recipe for meat loaf might outlast his high-priced styles. If he didn't fit the stereotype of the fashion designer—well, Bill Blass earned his success by playing by his own rules. Besotted with the glamour of the 1930s Hollywood movies of his Indiana boyhood, Blass came to New York City after World War II and began crafting his streamlined, modern look. After years as an apprentice, in 1970 he became one of the first U.S. designers to own his own label, and he built it into a powerhouse.

Blass believed that "a certain nonchalance is always a constant in American clothes," and his designs artfully merged the casual feel of sportswear with the elegance of high couture. His greatest advertisement, perhaps, was himself: handsome and debonair, well read and witty, he was the first designer to be welcomed into the wealthy circles of his clientele, whom he liked to call his "gals." They loved it.

SHELLY KATZ—TIMEPIX

Princess Margaret
1930-2002

She was born at Glamis Castle in Scotland—home to a famously troubled royal, Shakespeare's Macbeth—and her life played out as a tragedy, haunted by two failed love affairs. The younger sister of Britain's Queen Elizabeth, Princess Margaret was smart and witty, a bon vivant who loved café society and knew how to strike a pose with her trademark cigarette holder. But she never seemed to recover from her first love affair. At 22, she fell hard for a war hero, Group Captain Peter Townsend, but she was pressured not to marry him: he was divorced, and the royal family was still reeling from the abdication of Margaret's uncle, King Edward VIII, over his love affair with American divorcé Wallis Simpson.

In 1960 Margaret married a hip, motorcycle-riding photographer, Anthony Armstrong-Jones, who was given the title Lord Snowdon. They had two children, but Margaret found time to enjoy London in its mod heyday. When her husband focused on his career, Margaret took up with a would-be pop star 17 years her junior, Roddy Llewellyn, with whom she often spent time at her holiday home on the Caribbean island of Mustique. In 1978 she became the first British royal to be granted a divorce, a great irony after her affair with Townsend. A sad life? Perhaps. But as Louis Armstrong once told the British press, "Your Princess Margaret is one hip chick."

LORD SNOWDEN—CAMERA PRESS—RETNA

Milton Berle
1908-2002

His life is a history of 20th century show business: from movies to radio to television, Milton Berle was present at the creation of the century's major entertainment media. Child of a pushy stage mother, he first appeared onstage at the age of 5, and he was the baby tossed from a train in the early movie serial *The Perils of Pauline*. One of the great line of American Jewish comics, he conquered vaudeville, nightclubs and Broadway, and was the past master of the Friars Club roast. In 1948, he tried his hand in the new arena of television. His *Texaco Star Theater* was TV's first monster hit, emptying theaters and restaurants, and before long the hammy, ribald, fast-talking "Thief of Bad Gags" had a new handle: "Mr. Television."

Lisa Lopes
1972-2002

Too much, too soon? After Lisa (Left Eye) Lopes and her TLC bandmates Tionne Watkins and Rozonda Thomas became one of pop's biggest ever girl groups, Lopes' private life ran off the rails: she burned down her Atlanta mansion in a 1994 tiff with her boyfriend. Lopes died when she drove her car into a tree in Honduras.

Waylon Jennings
1937-2002

On the "day the music died"—Feb. 3, 1959—Buddy Holly's bass player was bumped from a plane flight that later crashed. Waylon Jennings put his second chance to good use: rebelling against Nashville's embrace of slick pop sounds, he joined with sidekick Willie Nelson to father country's unpolished, ornery "outlaw" movement. "You start messin' with my music, I get mean," the maverick said. Any doubters?

Sam Snead
1912-2002

Legendary? He won his first tournament in 1936 and his last in 1982. He grew up in Virginia, so poor his first clubs were fashioned out of tree limbs. Yet Sam Snead crafted what is still often described as the sweetest swing in the history of golf. Even his failures acquired a patina of myth: he was the first to win the Masters three times and also won three PGA championships, but "Slammin' Sam" never won the U.S. Open, and never seemed to stop hearing about it.

As he grew older, his swing endured: in 1979, Snead became the first PGA golfer to shoot his age—67—and he topped that with a 66 two days later. His fellow pros, who universally admired him (he played his first round with Tiger Woods when the phenom was only 6 years old), say his stories at the annual Masters champions dinner were … legendary.

John Entwistle
1944-2002

The still point in a turning world, John Entwistle was the quiet anchor of the seminal '60s British rock group the Who. In mid-storm, as Roger Daltrey twirled his mike, Pete Townshend windmilled his guitar riffs and Keith Moon manhandled his drum kit, Entwistle would stand "just like a statue," his long fingers producing astonishingly fleet, inventive runs on his bass guitar. Though not so prolific as chief songwriter Townshend, Entwistle wrote such slightly off-kilter Who classics as *My Wife* and the creepy *Boris the Spider*—to Townshend's amusement, always the most requested number at concerts.

Stalwart and stolid, Entwistle became known as "the Ox" and loaned the name to the band he led for years when the Who wasn't active. A creator of the "power pop" sound, he helped pioneer the rumbling music he termed "heavy metal," and he also gave his mates in Led Zeppelin their name. He died in Las Vegas the day before the Who were due to go on the road again.

THE KOBAL COLLECTION

MICHAEL PUTLAND—RETNA

Billy Wilder
1906-2002

It's official: Billy Wilder is the director of the funniest movie ever made in America. When the American Film Institute picked the best screen comedies of all time in 2000, *Some Like It Hot,* Wilder's 1959 tale of a pair of cross-dressing murder witnesses on the lam in an all-girl band was No. 1. But Wilder's genius wasn't confined to comedy: he is also the director of the classic, dark romance of early Hollywood, *Sunset Boulevard;* the gritty study of alcoholism *The Lost Weekend;* and the nifty noir thriller *Double Indemnity.*

Not a bad run for a Jewish immigrant from Austria who fled Nazi Germany and arrived in America in 1934 knowing only 100 words of English. A former newspaper reporter and always a scriptwriter at heart, Wilder worked best with a partner, collaborating first with the erudite Charles Brackett, then with his colleague of 30 years, I.A.L. (Izzy) Diamond. Wilder took up directing in the early 1940s when he grew impatient with Hollywood's treatment of his scripts. Frustrated when his later films failed to achieve success with audiences, he took solace in his collection of paintings by Picasso, Botero, Miró and others; he sold his works for more than $30 million in 1989. "I cannot say who is the greatest [filmmaker]," said an admirer, "but I can say that no one is greater than Billy Wilder." High praise indeed: the speaker was Federico Fellini.

Stephen Jay Gould
1941-2002

As science grows ever more technical and arcane, it desperately needs more popularizers, the gifted switch-hitters who are experts in their field—and experts in illuminating it for the general public. With his flair for memorable metaphors and everyday examples, Stephen Jay Gould was one of the best of the breed. A noted paleontologist, he shook up his field in the early 1970s when he and longtime colleague Niles Eldredge developed their theory of "punctuated equilibrium," which posits that evolution proceeds not in a smooth flow but in a series of fits and starts.

Gould was a fine writer who demystified science in dozens of books and in his long-running column in *Natural History,* which often digressed into another favorite topic, baseball (though Gould taught at Harvard University, he was born in New York City and remained a lifelong Yankees fan). His magnum opus, *The Structure of Evolutionary Theory,* was published months before he died.

WALLY MCNAMEE—CORBIS

Rosemary Clooney

1928-2002

The saucy, Kentucky-born singer began performing at 17 with her younger sister. She disdained her 1951 song *Come on-a My House*, but the hit launched her career, which included a fine turn opposite Bing Crosby in *White Christmas*. After her 1953 marriage to actor José Ferrer and the birth of their five children, she suffered a breakdown in 1968 that derailed her career. In the late 1970s she began to perform again; in recent years her warm, swinging cabaret performances won her a host of new fans—and a lifetime-achievement Grammy in 2002. (Trivia: she was the aunt, not the mother, of actor George Clooney.)

Paul Wellstone

1944-2002

The former college professor ran for the Senate from Minnesota in 1990 as a fiery rebel: of his new colleague Jesse Helms he said, "I have detested him since I was 19." Over nearly two Senate terms, Wellstone never wavered in his left-leaning convictions—no other member of the Senate was on the losing side of so many 99-to-1 or 98-to-2 votes—but he did adjust his style to the Senate's courtly atmosphere. Just how well he had adapted was evident after his campaign plane crashed only two weeks before the November election, killing Wellstone, his wife, daughter and five others. Despite their marked political differences, said a grieving Helms, "He was my friend. And I was his."

Jonas Savimbi

1934-2002

Savimbi, center, was the founder and longtime leader of UNITA, the Angolan rebel group that for 27 years fought the government in a civil war that claimed at least 500,000 lives. Savimbi, who studied medicine and political science in Europe and trained in guerrilla warfare in China, was gunned down in a firefight with the Angolan army. He became a U.S. ally in the cold war, fighting Angola's then-Marxist government. But he later isolated himself from his allies in the West when he rejected three peace deals and kept up the rebellion after losing a 1992 democratic presidential election. The rebel had not been seen for years before his death.

Cyrus Vance
1917-2002

Soft-spoken yet tough, the diplomat and onetime World War II gunnery officer played a pivotal role as President Jimmy Carter's Secretary of State. He helped normalize U.S. relations with China, win approval for the Panama Canal treaties and secure a peace accord between Egypt and Israel. He resigned in April 1980 over Carter's approval of a military operation to rescue hostages from Iran.

Chuck Jones
1912-2002

The master animator's cartoons were the star attractions of countless children's Saturday afternoons—and internal lives. But they were more than kid stuff. "We weren't making them for kids or for adults," he often said. "We were making them for ourselves." To salute him, we need only list the stock players that graced his seven-minute mini-masterpieces for Warner Bros.: Porky Pig, the harassed middle-management type; Elmer Fudd, the chronic, choleric dupe; Bugs Bunny, the cartoon Cagney—urban, crafty, pugnacious; Daffy Duck, modern man (well, modern mallard) in all his epic scheming and human frustration. And don't forget the bon-vivant skunk Pepe Le Pew, the beep-beep Road Runner and his perennially flummoxed pursuer, Wile E. Coyote. Kids always knew this stuff is funny. Connoisseurs now know it is great.

Peggy Lee
1920-2002

Her signature song was *Fever*, and that says all you need to know about Peggy Lee. Her subtle, insinuating way with a song took Norma Egstrom from 50¢-a-night gigs in small-town North Dakota to decades of success, first with Benny Goodman's band, then in recordings, film and TV. Writing in TIME, singer k.d. lang said, "I can't think of a better vocalist in that jazz-pop crooning style. What made her so good was that she interpreted and delivered songs with such a complex and dense range of emotions." Or, as jazz critic Leonard Feather quipped, "If you don't feel a thrill when Peggy Lee sings, you're dead, Jack."

Dudley Moore
1935-2002

He stood only 5 ft. 2 in., but Moore's droopy-eyed, droll manner made him an unlikely Hollywood heartthrob. A talented pianist, Moore was a veteran of Britain's great *Beyond the Fringe* troupe. His best roles were in the 1979 movie *10* and in 1981's *Arthur*, in which he played a sweet, wealthy drunk.

Otis Blackwell

Stephen Ambrose, 66, populist historian whose best-selling books, including 1992's *Band of Brothers* and 1994's *D-Day,* related the courage of citizen soldiers in World War II. Ambrose wrote 36 books, including biographies of Presidents Eisenhower and Nixon, but in 2001 he was criticized for failing to properly attribute other writers' words in some of them.

Walter Annenberg, 94, publishing magnate, philanthropist and art connoisseur who founded two hit magazines, *Seventeen* in 1944 and *TV Guide* in 1953. One of the world's wealthiest men, he served as U.S. ambassador to Britain under Richard Nixon.

Roone Arledge, 71, pioneering ABC executive whose technical innovations and show-biz flair reinvented TV news and sports. He introduced instant replay and slow motion, put Howard Cosell on the air, and strongly enhanced ABC's news coverage, creating *Nightline* to cover the Iran hostage crisis.

Otis Blackwell, 70, pioneering rock-'n'-roll tunesmith. Blackwell's memorable songs helped define the careers of Elvis Presley (*Don't Be Cruel, All Shook Up*), Jerry Lee Lewis (*Great Balls of Fire*), Peggy Lee (*Fever*) and James Taylor (*Handy Man*).

Joseph Bonanno, 97, don of one of New York City's five original Mafia families. He disliked his nickname, "Joe Bananas," and denied the Mafia ex-

isted. In his autobiography, he called himself a "venture capitalist."

Linda Boreman, 53, ex-pornography star best known by her screen moniker, Linda Lovelace. The heroine of 1972's classic *Deep Throat* published a 1980 autobiography, *Ordeal,* in which she charged that her abusive first husband forced her to take the role and that she made no money from it.

J. Carter Brown, 67, patrician populist. As head of Washington's National Gallery of Art, he helped transform museums from dusty vaults to extravagant showplaces for the masses.

James Coburn, 74, craggy, slyly intelligent Hollywood tough guy. His memorable villains were made creepier by his deep, satanic laugh and toothy, knowing grin. Among his best films were *The Magnificent Seven, The Great Escape* and *Major Dundee.* Sidelined by arthritis in the '80s, he won the Oscar for Best Supporting Actor in 1999 for his role in *Affliction.*

Abba Eban, 87, charismatic founding father of Israel. His skillful diplomacy and eloquent oratory helped build international support for the embattled nation. Resolutely dovish, he was an early advocate of a land-for-peace deal with the Palestinians.

Gregorio Fuentes, 104, Cuban fisherman, said to have inspired Ernest Hemingway's 1952 novella *The Old Man and the Sea.* In exchange for cash he would regale tourists with embellished reminiscences of "Papa," whose boat he skippered for some 20 years.

Lionel Hampton, 94, jazz vibraphonist. His effervescent performance style and masterly solo technique greatly extended jazz's popularity and turned him into one of the genre's few household names.

Nigel Hawthorne, 72, British stage and screen actor known for his role as a pompous, conniving civil servant in the '80s British television series *Yes, Minister.* Hawthorne scored a late-career triumph in the title role of *The Madness of King George.*

Thor Heyerdahl, 87, unorthodox Norwegian adventurer-anthropologist who in 1947 sailed the *Kon-Tiki,* a tiny balsa raft, from Peru to an island near Tahiti in an attempt to prove his controversial theory that the Polynesian Islands could have been settled by prehistoric Peruvians sailing west, not Southeast Asians sailing east.

Alexander Lebed, 52, blunt, charismatic Soviet general who led the defense of Russia's parliament in the 1991 coup attempt by communist hard-liners. He died in a helicopter crash.

Alan Lomax, 87, music collector who helped discover Woodie Guthrie, Jelly Roll Morton, Muddy Waters and others. Lomax brought American folk music to the world, influencing the British skiffle craze of the 1950s, which gave rise to the Quarrymen, led by a young John Lennon.

Stanley Marcus, 96, pioneering high-end retailer who transformed a family-run women's apparel store into the opulent Dallas-based emporium Neiman Marcus. He made his mark with the introduction of personalized gift wrapping, in-store fashion shows and a legendary line of extravagant his-and-her gifts, which once featured a pair of Beechcraft airplanes.

Jason Mizell, a.k.a. Jam Master Jay, 37, jovial DJ of the boundary-breaking rap group Run-D.M.C. Mizell was shot in his studio in Queens, N.Y., but the murder is a mystery: he was widely respected as rap's nicest guy

Stanley Marcus

and was an active member of his local community. Mizell was the first to fuse rap beats with rock melodies, fueling Run-D.M.C.'s historic crossover to mainstream turf and changing the sound of pop music forever.

Chaim Potok, 73, best-selling author of *The Chosen* and *My Name Is Asher Lev.* Potok gave mainstream readers a nuanced glimpse into the insular yet culturally rich community of Orthodox and Hasidic Jews, limning their struggle between religious devotion and love for the secular world. He was the son of Orthodox Polish immigrants who found his novels frivolous.

John Rawls, 81, gentle giant of liberalism. The Harvard professor changed the study of political philosophy from

Larry Rivers

one of logic and science to one concerned primarily with moral justice and the social contract.

Larry Rivers, 78, iconoclastic painter and sculptor who helped pave the way for the Pop Art movement by injecting ironic humor into the earnest, Abstract Expressionist–dominated art world of the 1950s. A saxophonist, writer and sometime actor, Rivers envisioned his obituary headline as GENIUS OF THE VULGAR DIES AT 63.

Howard K. Smith, 87, impassioned news broadcaster for CBS and ABC who in 1960 moderated the first televised presidential debate, between John F. Kennedy and Richard Nixon. Smith left CBS after clashing with its head

man, William Paley, over the network's timid coverage of civil rights strife.

Rod Steiger, 77, cuttingly intelligent actor who helped free stage and film performance from the kingdom of nice. Steiger often played icy, dominating tyrants—Napoleon, Al Capone, Mussolini—but won a Best Actor Oscar for 1967's *In the Heat of the Night,* which showed a warming trend.

Herman Talmadge, 88, cigar-chomping ex–U.S. Senator and Georgia Governor who got his start in politics as a staunch segregationist but later supported issues important to blacks. He lost his bid for a fifth term in 1980 after the Senate denounced him for financial improprieties.

Dave Thomas, 69, founder and playful pitchman for the Wendy's hamburger chain. Unable to find a decent burger in Columbus, Ohio, Thomas decided to make his own. He opened his first restaurant in 1969; today there are more than 6,000. Thomas, who was adopted, formed a foundation to support the practice. As a youngster, he bonded with his grandmother, who often told him, "Don't cut corners." Thus Wendy's square hamburger patties.

Pauline Trigere, 93, outspoken fashion diva whose elegant designs were worn by the Duchess of Windsor and Bette Davis. The first major designer to hire an African-American model, Trigere was generous—and blunt. She once clarified the upside of a low-cut dress by noting, "You can see the boobs better."

Johnny Unitas, 69, Hall of Fame quarterback who led the Baltimore Colts to a sudden-death victory over the New York Giants in the 1958 NFL championship game, still regarded by many as the greatest football game ever played. Teammate John Mackey once remarked of him, "It's like being in a huddle with God." Unitas' 47 consecutive games with a touchdown pass are still a league record.

Dave Van Ronk, 65, erudite folk, blues and jazz musician who was called the

Dave Thomas

Mayor of Greenwich Village during the folk revival of the '50s and '60s. His apartment was a gathering place for such famed musicians as Bob Dylan, Tom Paxton and Suzanne Vega.

Lew Wasserman, 89, the last of Hollywood's legendary movie moguls, who headed MCA, parent company of Universal Pictures, for four decades. A revolutionary, he broke the hold of tight studio contracts that locked up actors, embraced TV and, with *Jaws,* invented the summer blockbuster.

Byron White, 84, last surviving member of the Warren Supreme Court, who won renown first as football star "Whizzer" White, then as a defiantly independent jurist. He consistently supported civil rights but dissented in *Miranda v. Arizona,* which required police to read criminal suspects their rights, and sided with the antiabortion bloc in *Roe v. Wade.* ∎

Byron White